ISBN-13: 978-1468131918
ISBN-10: 1468131915

This book is dedicated to all my students over the past 10 years, I have learned just as much from all of you as you have learned from me.

I'd also like to acknowledge Larry Ronaldson and Robert Folatico, thank you for introducing me to the rewarding field of SAT tutoring.

Also, thank you to Derek Mauro and Alicia Oliva, your insight helped tremendously in making this book possible.

The 32 Most Effective SAT Math Strategies

A Proven Roadmap to Your First-Choice College

Steve Warner, Ph.D.

Table of Contents

iv

Actions to Complete Before You Read This Book

1. Purchase a TI-84 or equivalent calculator

It is recommended that you use a TI-84 or comparable calculator for the SAT. Answer explanations in this book will always assume you are using such a calculator.

2. Take a practice SAT from the Official Guide to get your preliminary SAT math score

Use this score to help you determine the problems you should be focusing on (see page 9 for details).

3. Download the Challenge Set

By purchasing this book you are entitled to the FREE downloadable book *Challenge Set #1*. To claim this book for FREE please visit the following webpage:

www.thesatmathprep.com/32SATch1.html

4. 'Like' my Facebook page

This is not essential, but I would really appreciate it. This page is filled with useful SAT math content. Visit the following webpage and click the 'like' button.

www.facebook.com/thesatmathprep

THE MINDSET TO MASTERING SAT MATH

SECRETS OF THE SAT

PREPARE SMARTER, NOT HARDER

*T*here are a few secrets every veteran SAT prep teacher knows. These secrets are something I've shared with every student I've tutored in the last 10 years.

If you understand these secrets you can go on to dramatically improve your score—often well beyond your highest expectations. And the best part is...many of these secrets have absolutely nothing to do with math.

But before I reveal these secrets to you, I want to make one thing clear: SAT math is *only* unfair to those who are not properly prepared. Many students believe that only gifted math students do well on the test. They're wrong. Other students believe you need to spend hundreds of hours preparing for the test to score well. They're also wrong.

A great SAT math score is all about *how* you prepare yourself. Fortunately for you, all preparation isn't created equal. By focusing on what's important you give yourself an advantage over every other student—and that's exactly what this book is going to do for you.

This book is written to give you the *maximum* result with the *minimum* effort. After 10 years of SAT math tutoring, I've boiled things down to the most important concepts and strategies. With just a small amount of preparation you can achieve a math score you will be proud of—easily.

More than anything else, the techniques from this book will train you to become a better problem solver. I will get you to think "outside the box," and to solve problems in more clever ways.

It may be "unfair" that better preparation will result in a higher score with less effort (and doing less actual math)—but why not let such unfairness work to your *advantage*? If you're ready to learn a whole new approach to SAT math, I'm ready to reveal the secrets and strategies that will catapult you over your classmates.

SECRET 1

YOU PROBABLY ALREADY KNOW ALL THE MATH NEEDED FOR THE TEST

*I*f you scored at least a 400 on the PSAT, then you most likely have all the mathematical knowledge needed to ace the SAT. It may help to review a few definitions and formulas, but knowing more math *won't* boost your score very much.

For those with a PSAT score below a 400, fear not. Your mathematical vocabulary just needs some work—which we'll cover in this book. Pay special attention to the definitions when reviewing problems and you'll be all set.

Ironically, students already taking Calculus sometimes have the most difficulty remembering the basic definitions. It's nothing to worry about though—just make sure not to go into the SAT cold. Do the practice problems included with this book so you remember the basic terms you may have forgotten.

So, rather than learn more math, you can drastically increase your score by following simple strategies that have nothing to do with your mathematical ability, such as:

- Reduce the number of questions you answer
- Guess more strategically
- Make minor adjustments in your study habits

These are all strategies we're going to cover in this introduction.

Moreover, there are many question-specific strategies you can use to get answers quicker, make problems easier to understand, and get answers in ways you probably never considered. We'll cover these strategies in the main part of the book. Remember, it's all about becoming a better *problem solver*—not a better mathematician.

The SAT isn't actually testing you on math—even if the "language" is math. Instead, you're being tested on your problem solving skills and reasoning abilities. The test makers include questions that are intentionally designed to trick students so that those clever enough to identify these "tricks" score higher and standout.

Think of it this way: colleges aren't necessarily looking for gifted mathematicians. Colleges are looking for creative and innovative thinkers—students who can find unique solutions to problems. This is why better preparation leads to better scores. By preparing with this book, you're focusing on what's important and learning how to identify and solve tricky problems so that you score higher and stand out from your classmates.

SECRET 2
GAINING MATHEMATICAL MATURITY

*W*hile knowing more math *won't* increase your score, sometimes learning certain *types* of math can increase your level of mathematical maturity. This *will* improve your score. Students taking AP Calculus usually have a higher level of mathematical maturity than a student in remedial algebra. As such, the AP Calc student is more likely to do better in math on the SAT.

There is no strict measure of mathematical maturity, but let's examine what various levels of mathematical maturity might look like:

Level	Ability	Description
1	Can do basic high school math when taught in a classroom setting	Students at level 1 can do basic algebra and geometry by following the procedures that were taught to them. If such a student were asked, "Why does this work?" they will not be able to verbalize a satisfactory answer. **Most high school students are at this level.**

2	Can learn basic mathematics on own	This student can read an algebra or precalculus book and answer the questions at the end of the chapter with great success, and can probably explain basic mathematics to other students. If shown how to do a problem, they will be able to solve problems that are similar using the same strategy. **This student would have no problem in a Calculus course.**
3	Can learn advanced mathematics on own	This student can not only do problems, but can also explain why the methods work. They can often solve problems in several different ways and develop their own techniques for solving problems. **This student will be able to solve problems of a type that they have never seen before as long as they know the appropriate definitions and relevant background material.**

These "levels" are just here to illustrate a point. It's often hard to pinpoint the exact level of a student. Some students naturally have a higher level of mathematical maturity than others.

The good news is that mathematical maturity can be increased. Doing so will greatly improve your problem solving ability as well as increase your math score on the SAT. Here are a few ways you can increase your level of mathematical maturity.

1. **Do SAT math problems.** If you can currently only solve Level 1 geometry problems, and a month from now you can solve Level 2 geometry problems, then guess what—*you've increased your level of mathematical maturity.* So keep doing SAT problems a level above your current ability until the day of the test. If you only have about 3 months before your test, then this is the method you should employ most, if not exclusively.

2. **Learn some mathematics by yourself.** This may seem contrary to what has already been stated—but it's not. *Knowing* more mathematics will probably not raise your score very much, especially if the math is handfed to you. But the process of *learning* mathematics will increase your mathematical maturity. What kind of math should you learn? *It doesn't matter!* Pick something you find the most enjoyable, and try to learn it on your own. If you get stuck, then ask for help—but developing the skill to learn math yourself will definitely increase your mathematical maturity. This strategy is more long term and you should consider it if you have 6 months or more before your SAT exam.

3. **Attempt difficult math problems.** There are a lot of challenging math problems out there that *only* require the math that you already know. There are math magazines, websites, and books full of problems. Pick a few and struggle with them. Just trying difficult problems and developing strategies will increase your mathematical maturity, even if you never solve a single one on your own. Don't forget to attempt the "challenge problems" at my website. These problems were specifically created to boost your level of mathematical maturity.

You can use this book to increase your SAT score without increasing your mathematical skill by just learning some or all of the given strategies; however, if you want to do *even better*, use this book to also increase your level of mathematical maturity. To do this, do each problem over and over—first become comfortable applying the given strategy for the section, and then try doing the problem *without* using the given strategy. On the actual SAT you should always use the technique that gets you the answer the quickest (and with which you're most comfortable), but attacking problems in different ways during practice will make you a better mathematician.

Finally, if you want to really improve your level of mathematical maturity, then instead of just solving each problem, try to *understand* why the method you're using works. I'll explain why methods work throughout the book, often after the heading, "For the advanced student." These sections are purely optional, but if and when you're ready to study them, they can really make you a much better problem solver.

If this is too sophisticated for you, don't worry. You're not alone. You can still improve your score just by learning the simple and easy-to-follow strategies in this book.

How I Developed Mathematical Maturity

I can still remember the day I got back my first real analysis homework as a first year graduate student at Rutgers University. I received a 62. This is by far the lowest grade I had ever received in mathematics. The worst part was that I had spent many hours on this homework, and I thought that it was completely correct.

I remember approaching my teacher explaining that I never received such a low math grade, begging for him to tell me what to do. But he didn't have an answer for me. I was on my own.

That whole first year of graduate school was a struggle. I wound up with B's in most of my classes despite working harder than I had ever worked in my life. I was unprepared for how difficult graduate school was, especially after receiving a 4.0 Math GPA as an undergraduate with very little effort.

This was quite disheartening and I thought that there was no way I would be able to do mathematical research and get my Ph.D. I just wasn't smart enough.

14

But an interesting thing happened during my second year. Apparently my hard work paid off. All of a sudden nothing seemed difficult anymore—I was back at the top of my class. Despite the fact that I was taking even harder classes than the previous year I was breezing through them with very little effort.

All of a sudden I was able to read advanced graduate texts on my own and do the problems at the end of each section without any help from others. *What happened?* Did I all of a sudden accumulate a massive amount of mathematical knowledge. The answer is no. In fact, this wouldn't have helped. The mathematical language in my new classes was actually quite different from what I had learned the previous year.

What happened is that by struggling so hard the year before with little to no help from others, I managed to increase my level of mathematical maturity. Things that I didn't stand a chance of understanding just a year earlier now made perfect sense. Other students were now coming to me for help, and I was able to help every single one of them. To think just a year earlier I was considering dropping out because it was just too hard. What a shame that would have been.

My level of mathematical maturity had to take several more jumps before I would graduate. Mathematical research is highly sophisticated and requires a clever mind that is willing to think in unconventional ways. The one thing that my years at graduate school have taught me is that anyone is capable of doing anything that they set their mind to.

Just don't give up and you will persevere!

SECRET 3
THE RIGHT WAY TO PREPARE: THE BEST 8 THINGS TO DO BEFORE THE TEST

*B*efore you even open the SAT booklet, here are the 8 best ways you can prepare yourself for the test.

1. Redoing problems that you get wrong.

If you get a problem wrong, and never attempt the problem again, then it's extremely unlikely that you will get a similar problem correct if it appears on the SAT.

Most students will read an explanation of the solution, or have someone explain it to them (if they have a tutor or are taking a course), and then never look at the problem again. This is *not* how you optimize your SAT score. To be sure that you will get a similar problem correct on the SAT, you must get the problem correct before the SAT—and without actually remembering the problem.

This means that after getting a problem incorrect, you should go over and understand why you got it wrong, wait at least a few days, then attempt the same problem again. If you get it right you can cross it off your list of problems to review. If you get it wrong, keep revisiting it every few days until you get it right.

Your score does not improve by getting problems correct. Your score improves when you learn from your mistakes. This is something that is pretty obvious but somehow overlooked.

2. Take practice tests as you would take the real test.

If you don't take your practice tests the same way you take the actual SAT, then you may very well forget to do some very important things on the actual test. All of the strategies in this book should be implemented every time you take a practice test.

3. Practice problems of the appropriate level.

Roughly speaking about 1/3 of the math problems on the SAT are easy, 1/3 are medium, and 1/3 are hard. If you answer 2/3 of the math questions on the SAT correctly, then your score will be approximately a 600 (out of 800). That's right—you can get about a 600 on the math portion of the SAT without answering a single hard question.

What this means to you depends on your current math ability. If you're a student that scored a 400 on your PSAT, then this is pretty good news. If you scored a 650 on your PSAT then perhaps it's not as exciting.

Keep track of your current ability level so that you know the types of problems you should focus on. If you're currently scoring around a 400 on your practice tests, then you should not be focusing on hard questions. You can easily raise your score 100 points without having to practice a single hard problem. Your focus should be on easy and medium problems.

If you are currently scoring about a 500, then you will want to work on some hard problems and some easy ones, but mostly medium level problems. And don't worry about the really hard ones—not until your score goes up at least another hundred points.

If you're scoring around a 600, it's time to start working on those harder problems. But, at the same time, you should learn some of the more advanced timesaving techniques for the easy and medium problems. This way you'll have more time during the test to focus on those harder ones.

Those of you at the 700 level really need to practice those problems that appear at the very end of each section. And if you're going for an 800, then you may want to work on some problems that are a little bit harder than actual SAT problems.

If you really want to refine your studying, then you should keep track of your ability level in each of the four major categories of problems:

1. **Number Theory**
2. **Algebra and Functions**
3. **Probability, Statistics and Data Analysis**
4. **Geometry**

For example, many students have trouble with very easy geometry problems, even though they can do more difficult number theory problems. This type of student may want to focus on easy and medium geometry questions, but medium and hard number theory questions.

It may seem a bit tedious to worry about such things, but even having just a vague idea of where you stand in each topic could be helpful. The main point here is don't waste your time practicing problems that you don't even plan to attempt on the SAT.

4. Practice every single day...but just a little.

Ideally you want to practice doing SAT math problems 10-20 minutes each day beginning at least 3 months before the exam. The only exception is on a day you do a practice test. You should do at least four practice tests before you take the SAT. Ideally you should do your practice tests on a Saturday or Sunday morning. At first you can do just the 3 math sections (of course if you are preparing for critical reading and writing as well, then you can do the whole test). The last one or two times you take a practice test you should do the whole test in one sitting. As tedious as this is, it will prepare you for the amount of endurance that it will take to get through this exam.

So what's the difference if you do 10-20 minutes a day every day, or two hours in one sitting once a week? *Retention.* You tend to remember the first few things you learn and the last few things you learn. So you want to keep the middle as short as possible. You will retain much more of what you study if you study in short bursts than if you try to tackle everything at once.

18

So try to choose about a 20 minute block of time that you will dedicate to SAT math every night (and if you only need 10 or 15 on a particular night, that's ok). Make it a habit—this is *not* optional.

5. Do not study the day before the test.

If you have been studying the proper way for 3 months before the test, then you can relax the day before you take the test. Get a good night's sleep. It's unlikely that you will learn anything on this one day that will raise your score.

6. Enjoy the process.

Studying for the SAT does not have to be tedious. While studying for this test you're learning to be a better problem solver, increasing your level of mathematical maturity, and you might even learn some mathematics. Just doing a few problems a day for 10 to 20 minutes can make all the difference in the world.

7. Quick warm up the morning before the test.

The morning of the test do about 5 math problems that are not too difficult for you. The purpose is not to learn more math — it's just to put your mind into the correct state.

8. Know the geometric formulas that are given to you.

You should actually memorize these formulas. Why waste time flipping back and forth to these formulas? There aren't that many. So just learn them.

If for some reason you're not sure if you remember a formula correctly while taking the test, then by all means flip to the front of the section and take a look at the formula. But think about how quick and easy this will be if you are already very familiar with the formula.

In particular, become familiar with the two special triangles. Questions that use these are generally hard problems—that is, they appear toward the end of the section. But they are not difficult if you simply know how to use these triangles properly.

There are a few other formulas that you should have memorized before taking the SAT. The important ones appear in this book.

You should, of course, also memorize the directions for each section. Never read these during the test. That would be a serious waste of your time.

Notes:

(1) The advice from this section applies to using this book as well. You **do not** need to understand everything presented here to raise your score. For example, if you're currently scoring around a 400 in math on practice tests, then you don't need to worry too much about the harder problems. So don't take the Level 4 and 5 problems too seriously right now. Focus on Levels 1 through 3. You can come back to those harder questions later after your score improves a bit.

(2) Most problems in this book are solved in several different ways. The first solution always uses the strategy that is the title of that section. Many students have requested that I just tell them the solution that will get the answer as quickly as possible. For each problem, this quick solution is marked with an asterisk (*) right before the bold face header. Keep in mind that this particular solution may or may not be easy to understand. Only very advanced students should worry about focusing on these quick solutions.

SECRET 4
THE RIGHT WAY TO PREPARE: THE BEST 12 THINGS TO DO DURING THE TEST

*N*ote: *Every tip mentioned in this section should be followed every time you take a practice SAT as well as on the actual test. If you haven't trained yourself with these behaviors beforehand, it's extremely unlikely that you will use these behaviors when you take the actual exam.*

1. Leave at least 5 minutes towards the end of each section to check over easier problems.

It doesn't matter if you haven't finished the section. The last few problems on each math section are very difficult. If you have to leave some of these blank, then it's ok. It's better to spend your time looking for careless errors on problems that you can do than it is to waste your time on tricky problems that you are likely to get wrong. If you catch even one careless error per math section, your score can potentially go up *40 points.*

You should make sure that you are wearing a watch during the exam, of course.

2. Know the proper way to "check" your answers.

When you go back to check your earlier answers for careless errors *do not* simply look over your work to try to catch a mistake. This is usually a waste of time. Always redo the problem without looking at any of your previous work. Ideally, you want to use a different method than you used the first time.

For example, if you solved the problem by picking numbers the first time, try to solve it algebraically the second time, or at the very least pick different numbers. If you don't know, or are not comfortable with a different method, then use the same method, but do the problem from the beginning and do not look at your original solution. If your two answers don't match up, then you know that this a problem you need to spend a little more time on to figure out where your error is.

This may seem time consuming, but that's ok. It's better to spend more time checking over a few problems, then to rush through a lot of problems and repeat the same mistakes.

3. The art of guessing.

Answering a multiple choice question wrong results in a 1/4 point penalty. This is to discourage random guessing. If you have no idea how to do a problem, no intuition as to what the correct answer might be, and you can't even eliminate a single answer choice, then *DO NOT* just take a guess. Omit the question and move on.

If, however, you can eliminate even one answer choice, you should take a guess from the remaining four. You should of course eliminate as many choices as you can before you take your guess.

You are not penalized for getting a grid-in question wrong. Therefore you should always guess on grid-in questions that you don't know. Never leave any of these blank. If you have an idea of how large of a number the answer should be, then take a reasonable guess. If not, then just guess anything—don't think too hard—just put in a number.

4. How many questions should you attempt?

There are 3 math sections on the SAT. They can appear in any order. There is a 20 question multiple choice section, a 16 question multiple choice section, and an 18 question section that has 8 multiple choice questions and 10 grid-ins.

Let's call these sections A, B, and C, respectively. You should first make sure that you know what you got on your last SAT practice test, actual

SAT, or actual PSAT (whichever you took last). What follows is a general goal you should go for when taking the exam.

Score	Section A	Section B	Section C (Multiple choice)	Section C (Grid-in)
< 330	7/20	6/16	2/8	2/10
330 – 370	10/20	8/16	3/8	3/10
380 – 430	12/20	10/16	4/8	4/10
440 – 490	14/20	11/16	5/8	6/10
500 – 550	16/20	12/16	6/8	8/10
560 – 620	18/20	15/16	7/8	9/10
630 – 800	20/20	16/16	8/8	10/10

For example, a student with a current score of 450 should attempt the first 14 questions from section A, the first 11 questions from section B, the first 5 multiple choice questions from section C, and the first 6 grid-ins from section C.

This is *just* a general guideline. Of course it can be fine tuned. As a simple example, if you are particularly strong at number theory problems, but very weak at geometry problems, then you may want to try every number theory problem no matter where it appears, and you may want to reduce the number of geometry problems you attempt.

5. Relax—it's just a test.

If you don't do as well as you would like the first time, it's *not* the end of the world. You can take the test multiple times and many colleges will focus on your best scores. Also, the SAT is just one of many factors that a college uses in its decisions. So take the test seriously during the months before when you are preparing so that you can get the best score possible. But when test day comes, just go in there, relax, and do the best that you can.

6. Pace yourself.

Do not waste your time on a question that is too hard or will take too long. After you've been working on a question for about 1 minute you need to make a decision. If you understand the question and think that you can get the answer in another 30 seconds or so, continue to work on the problem. If you still don't know how to do the problem or you're using a technique that is going to take a long time, mark it off and come back to it later if you have time.

If you have eliminated at least one answer choice, or it is a grid-in, feel free to take a guess. But you still want to leave open the possibility of coming back to it later. Remember that every problem is worth the same amount. Don't sacrifice problems that you may be able to do by getting hung up on a problem that is too hard for you.

7. Mark questions that you need to come back to clearly.

If you are pacing yourself properly, then you will probably skip some questions that you may want to come back to if you have time. Make sure you mark these questions clearly so that you can get back to them quickly when it is appropriate to do so.

Also, be very careful when filling in answers that you're filling in the answer for the correct question number. Be especially careful when you're skipping questions.

8. Use but don't abuse your calculator.

You should definitely use your calculator for computations that would take longer by hand such as simple computations involving addition, subtraction, multiplication, division, exponentiation, and taking roots. You can also sometimes use the graphing capabilities of your calculator to solve certain problems, although very often this may take longer than other methods.

While we're on the subject of calculators, please make sure that your calculator has fresh batteries the day of the test. Nobody will supply one for you if yours dies. Also make sure that you are using a calculator that you are very comfortable with. Ideally you should have just one calculator that you use whenever you are practicing SAT Math problems, and this should be the same calculator that you bring with you on test day. When a problem in this book has a solution using a calculator in its explanation it will be assumed that a TI-84 or comparable calculator is being used.

9. Never truncate or round calculator computations until the end of the problem.

If you are doing computations on your calculator always try to use the answer that your calculator has given to do later computations. Keep in mind that there is an ANS button on your calculator that uses the answer that your calculator produced last. Rounding or truncating too soon can lead to an incorrect final answer.

10. The proper way to write your answer on grid-in questions.

The computer only grades what you have marked in the bubbles. The space above the bubbles is just for your convenience, and to help you do your bubbling correctly.

Never mark more than one circle in a column or the problem will automatically be marked wrong. You do not need to use all four columns. If you don't use a column just leave it blank.

11. What you can and can't answer on grid-ins.

The symbols that you can grid in are the digits 0 through 9, a decimal point, and a division symbol for fractions. Note that there is no negative symbol. So answers to grid-ins *cannot* be negative. Also, there are only four slots, so you can't get an answer such as 52,326.

Sometimes there is more than one correct answer to a grid-in question. Simply choose one of them to grid-in. *Never* try to fit more than one answer into the grid.

If your answer is a whole number such as 2451 or a decimal that only requires four or less slots such as 2.36, then simply enter the number starting at any column. The two examples just written must be started in the first column, but the number 16 can be entered starting in column 1, 2 or 3.

Note that there is no zero in column 1, so if your answer is 0 it must be gridded into column 2, 3 or 4.

Fractions can be gridded in any form as long as there are enough slots. The fraction 2/100 must be reduced to 1/50 simply because the first representation won't fit in the grid.

Fractions can also be converted to decimals before being gridded in. If a decimal cannot fit in the grid, then you can simply *truncate* it to fit. But you must use every slot in this case. For example, the decimal .167777777... can be gridded as .167, but .16 or .17 would both be marked wrong.

Instead of truncating decimals you can also *round* them. For example, the decimal above could be gridded as .168. Truncating is preferred because there is no thinking involved and you are less likely to make a careless error.

Here are three ways to grid in the number 8/9.

Never grid-in mixed numerals. If your answer is 2 ¼, and you grid in the mixed numeral 2 ¼, then this will be read as 21/4 and will be marked wrong. You must either grid in the decimal 2.25 or the improper fraction 9/4.

Here are two ways to grid in the mixed numeral 1 ½ correctly.

12. Time is not as much of an issue as you think.

Remember that you don't need to attempt all of the problems unless your current ability level is a 630 or higher. If you stick to the number of suggested problems above, then you will have plenty of time during the test to do the allotted number of problems carefully and to check many of them over.

Don't stress out over time. This is counterproductive and the fact is that if you're taking the test right there is plenty of time.

SAT MYTHS
THE 4 STRATEGIES THAT DO NOT WORK

You may have gotten advise from various sources on test-taking in general, and the SAT. Here are some common pieces of advice that you should *not* follow.

1. When in doubt choose choice (C).

This strategy does not work on the SAT (and it's unlikely to work on any standardized test). The test is carefully created so that all answer choices are equally likely. Remember that you should only take a guess on multiple choice questions if you can eliminate at least *one* answer choice. At this point feel free to choose (C) if it has not been eliminated, but there certainly isn't any advantage to doing so.

2. Go with your first instinct.

This strategy is ok for the first few problems in any given section, since they are meant to be easy and straightforward. But medium and especially hard questions are designed to trick you. Therefore, your first instinct may very well be to fall into the exact trap they have set for you.

You should be especially cautious if your "intuition" gets you an answer very quickly on one of the higher numbered problems in a section. Following the technique of quasi-elimination (this will be detailed a bit later) you should actually eliminate this choice and possibly take a guess among the remaining choices.

3. The best way to study for the SAT is by doing lots of practice tests.

Although taking practice tests is not a bad thing, it is not the most efficient way to increase your performance on the SAT. The best way to increase your SAT score is by *doing just a few SAT problems a day over a period of several months.*

Taking a practice test will be most effective if you make sure that you go over all the problems that you got wrong, understand your mistakes, and (most importantly) you periodically redo the problems you got wrong until you can do each one yourself without referring back to the solution.

When doing this, remember to focus on problems that are within and slightly above your current ability level. If you're struggling with Level 2 geometry problems, then you shouldn't be worrying about Level 4 and 5 geometry problems at all.

I am by no means implying that you should not take any practice tests. You should take at least four before the actual exam (as stated above), but this is not the time that you are improving your mathematical and reasoning ability.

4. Take the test during an "off" month because it's easier.

There is no evidence that suggests that you will get a better score on the SAT if you take it in one month as opposed to another month. Take the SAT when you are ready, preferably after you have done at least three months of consistent preparation. Try to take the test for the first time in your junior year.

THE TACTICS FOR MASTERING SAT MATH

STRATEGY 1
START WITH CHOICE (C)

*I*n many problems you can get the answer simply by trying each of the answer choices until you find the one that works. Unless you have some intuition as to what the correct answer might be, then you should always start with choice (C) as your first guess (an exception will be detailed in the next strategy). The reason for this is simple. Answers are usually given in increasing or decreasing order. So very often if choice (C) fails you can eliminate two of the other choices as well.

This is not always the most efficient way to do a problem, but it is a method that will often get you the answer without too much effort.

LEVEL 1: NUMBER THEORY

1. Three consecutive integers are listed in increasing order. If their sum is 531, what is the second integer in the list?

   (A) 176
   (B) 177
   (C) 178
   (D) 179
   (E) 180

Begin by looking at choice (C). If the second integer is 178, then the first integer is 177 and the third integer is 179. Therefore we get a sum of 177 + 178 + 179 = 534. This is a little too big. So we can eliminate choices (C), (D) and (E).

We next try choice (B). If the second integer is 177, then the first integer is 176 and the third integer is 178. So the sum is 176 + 177 + 178 = 531. Thus, the answer is choice (B).

Remark 1: You should use your calculator to compute these sums. This will be quicker and you are less likely to make a careless error.

Remark 2: This method is faster than solving the problem algebraically. You don't have to show your work on this test so it's usually best to avoid algebra when possible.

* A quick, clever solution: A really sharp math student might realize that you can get the answer to this problem very quickly by dividing 531 by 3.

An algebraic solution: This method is **not** recommended for the SAT! We include it for the more advanced student that wants an actual solution to the problem that doesn't involve any tricks. If we name the least integer x, then the second and third integers are x +1 and x + 2, respectively. So we have

$$x + (x + 1) + (x + 2) = 531$$
$$3x + 3 = 531$$
$$3x = 528$$
$$x = 176$$

The second integer is $x + 1 = 177$, choice (B).

Important: Always remember to check what the question is asking for before choosing your answer. Many students would accidently choose choice (A) here as soon as they discovered that $x = 176$.

Note: The following is a bit more efficient.

$$x + (x + 1) + (x + 2) = 531$$
$$3x + 3 = 531$$
$$3(x + 1) = 531$$
$$x + 1 = 177$$

This also shows why the clever solution above gives the correct answer.

Definitions: The **integers** are the counting numbers together with their negatives.

$$\{...,-4, -3, -2, -1, 0, 1, 2, 3, 4,...\}$$

Consecutive integers are integers that follow each other in order. The difference between consecutive integers is 1. Here are two examples.

1, 2, 3   these are three consecutive integers
-3, -2, -1, 0, 1   these are five consecutive integers

In general, if x is an integer, then x, $x + 1$, $x + 2$, $x + 3$, ... are consecutive integers.

Interesting fact: In a set of consecutive integers, the average (arithmetic mean) and median are equal.

LEVEL 2: ALGEBRA

2. If $5^{y+1} = 625$, what is the value of y ?

    (A) 6
    (B) 5
    (C) 4
    (D) 3
    (E) 2

Begin by looking at choice (C). We substitute 4 in for y in the given equation. We type it in our calculator as 5^(4 + 1) = 3125. This number is too large, so we can eliminate choices (A), (B) and (C). We next try choice (D). 5^(3 + 1) = 625. Thus, the answer is choice (D).

Calculator note: When doing a calculator computation involving an exponent, always put the exponent in parentheses (if the exponent is just a single number, then it's ok to omit the parentheses, but you will still get the correct answer if you put the parentheses in).

In general, there are 4 instances when you should use parentheses in your calculator.

    (1) Around numerators of fractions
    (2) Around denominators of fractions
    (3) Around exponents
    (4) Whenever you actually see parentheses in the expression

Examples:

We will substitute a 3 in for x in each of the following examples.

Expression	Calculator computation
$\dfrac{3x+1}{5x-2}$	(3*3 + 1)/(5*3 − 2)
$(4x-3)^{4x-7}$	(4*3 − 3)^(4*3 − 7)

One more calculator note: Instead of typing 5^(3 + 1) in our calculator, we can add 3 and 1 in our head (to get 4), and type 5^4 instead. Notice that no parentheses are needed for a single number. You will get the correct answer however if you use parentheses, ie. if you type 5^(4).

An algebraic solution for the advanced student: We rewrite the equation so that both sides have the same base (in this case the common base is 5). $5^{y+1} = 5^4$. Now that the bases are the same, so are the exponents. So, y + 1 = 4, and therefore y = 3. The answer is choice (D).

* Finger counting: Use your fingers as you keep multiplying by five:

$$5, 25, 125, 625.$$

In this way we see that $5^4 = 625$, and therefore y = 3, choice (D).

LEVEL 3: ALGEBRA

3. A small hotel has 30 rooms which are all occupied. If each room is occupied by either one or two guests and there are 40 guests in total, how many rooms are occupied by two guests?

     (A) 14
     (B) 13
     (C) 12
     (D) 11
     (E) 10

Begin by looking at choice (C). If 12 rooms are occupied by 2 guests, then there are 30 − 12 = 18 rooms that are occupied by one guest. So the total number of guests is 12 * 2 + 18 * 1 = 24 + 18 = 42. This is too many guests, so there must be **fewer** rooms with two guests. We can therefore eliminate choices (A), (B) and (C).

We next try choice (D). If 11 rooms are occupied by 2 guests, then there are 30 − 11 = 19 rooms that are occupied by one guest. So the total number of guests is 11*2 + 19*1 = 22 + 19 = 41.

This is still too many guests, and so the answer must be choice (E).

Let's just confirm that the answer is in fact choice (E). If 10 rooms are occupied by 2 guests, then there are 30 − 10 = 20 rooms that are occupied by one guest. Therefore, we have that the total number of guests is 10*2 + 20*1 = 20 + 20 = 40. This confirms that choice (E) is the correct answer.

* A quick solution: Put one guest into each room. This takes care of 30 guests. There are 40 − 30 = 10 guests left. Therefore 10 rooms must have two guests, choice (E).

An algebraic solution: This method is **not** recommended for the SAT! We are including it for the more advanced student that wants an actual solution to the problem that doesn't involve any tricks. Let's let x be the number of rooms occupied by one guest, and y the number of rooms occupied by two guests. Since there are 30 rooms in total, we must have that x + y = 30. We also have x + 2y = 40 because there are 40 students in total. So we have the following system of equations.

$$x + 2y = 40$$
$$x + y = 30$$

We will use the **elimination method**. Note that we want to find y. We will therefore eliminate x. We can do this quickly by subtracting the bottom equation from the top one.

$$x + 2y = 40$$
$$\underline{x + y = 30}$$
$$y = 10$$

Thus, the answer is choice (E).

LEVEL 2: GEOMETRY

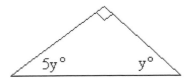

Note: Figure not drawn to scale.

4. In the right triangle above, what is the value of y ?

    (A) 15
    (B) 18
    (C) 21
    (D) 30
    (E) 60

We begin with choice (C). So we let y = 21. Then 5y = 105.

$$90 + 21 + 105 = 216.$$

Since 216 > 180 we can eliminate choice (C), as well as choices (D) and (E). Let's try choice (A) next. So we let y = 15. Then 5y = 75.

$$90 + 15 + 75 = 180$$

Therefore (A) is the correct answer.

* A quick algebraic solution: 5y + y must be equal to 90. So 6y = 90, and therefore y = 90/6 = 15, choice (A).

LEVEL 4: NUMBER THEORY

5. A ball is dropped from 1215 centimeters above the ground and after the fourth bounce it rises to a height of 15 centimeters. If the height to which the ball rises after each bounce is always the same fraction of the height reached on its previous bounce, what is this fraction?

(A) $\dfrac{1}{81}$

(B) $\dfrac{1}{27}$

(C) $\dfrac{1}{9}$

(D) $\dfrac{1}{3}$

(E) $\dfrac{1}{2}$

* Let's begin with choice (C). We divide 1215 by 9 four times and get 0.1851851852 which is much too small. So we can eliminate choices (A), (B) and (C). We next try choice (D). If we divide 1215 by 3 four times we get 15 so that (D) is the correct answer.

Note: We could have also multiplied 15 by 3 four times to get 1215.

A remark about difficulty: Since this is a Level 4 problem it is considered somewhat hard. This means that many students got it wrong on an experimental section of the SAT and so we may be able to eliminate certain choices with about 95% certainty. I call this process **quasi-elimination.** In this problem we could quasi-eliminate choice (A) because 15/1215 = 1/81. This simple computation can be done quickly in your calculator and therefore it would be "too easy" for a hard problem. The topic of quasi-elimination will be covered in more detail below. Note that quasi-elimination only works in **hard** problems (Level 4 or 5).

An algebraic solution for the advanced student: We want to solve the following equation.

$$1215x^4 = 15$$
$$x^4 = 15/1215 = 1/81$$
$$x = 1/3$$

Thus, the answer is choice (D).

LEVEL 4: GEOMETRY

6. When each side of a given square is lengthened by 3 inches, the area is increased by 45 square inches. What is the length, in inches, of a side of the original square?

   (A) 3
   (B) 4
   (C) 5
   (D) 6
   (E) 7

* Let's begin with choice (C). If the original length of a side of the square is 5, then the length becomes 8 when we increase it by 3. The area of the original square is 5*5 = 25 and the new square has area 8*8 = 64. So the area is increased by 64 − 25 = 39 square inches. So we can eliminate choice (C), and most likely (A) and (B) as well. We next try choice (D). 6*6 = 36, 9*9 = 81 and 81 − 36 = 45. Thus, the answer is choice (D).

An algebraic solution for the advanced student: Let x be the length, in inches, of a side of the original square. The length of a side of the new square is x + 3. The area of the original square is x^2, and the area of the new square is $(x + 3)^2 = (x + 3)(x + 3) = x^2 + 6x + 9$.

$$(x^2 + 6x + 9) − x^2 = 45$$
$$6x + 9 = 45$$
$$6x = 36$$
$$x = 6$$

Thus, the answer is choice (D).

STRATEGY 2
WHEN NOT TO START WITH CHOICE (C)

*I*f the word **least** appears in the problem, then start with the smallest number as your first guess. Similarly, if the word **greatest** appears in the problem, then start with the largest number as your first guess.

LEVEL 1: NUMBER THEORY

7. What is the least positive integer divisible by the integers 2, 3, 6 and 7?

    (A) 168
    (B) 126
    (C) 84
    (D) 42
    (E) 28

Begin by looking at choice (E) since it is the smallest. 28/2 = 14 and so 28 is divisible by 2. But 28/3 comes to approximately 9.33 in our calculator. Since this is not an integer, 28 is not divisible by 3. We can therefore eliminate choice (E). We next try choice (D).

$$42/2 = 21 \quad 42/3 = 14 \quad 42/6 = 7 \quad 42/7 = 6$$

Thus, the answer is choice (D).

Note: If we were to begin with choice (C) we would see that 84 is divisible by the four given integers. We could then eliminate choices (A) and (B), but we do not know if (C) is the answer.

Remark: Since 6 is divisible by 2 and 3, we only actually have to check divisibility by 6 and 7. In fact, the problem is actually asking for the **least common multiple** of 2, 3, 6 and 7 which is 2*3*7 = 42.

Remark for the more advanced student: Here is a quick way to find the least common multiple of a set of positive integers (we will use the four integers in the problem as an example).

Step 1: Find the prime factorization of each integer in the set.

$$2 = 2$$
$$3 = 3$$
$$6 = 2*3$$
$$7 = 7$$

Step 2: Choose the highest power of each prime that appears in any of the factorizations.

2, 3 and 7 (in this example the highest power of each prime is 1)

Step 3: Multiply these numbers together to get the least common multiple.

$$2*3*7 = 42$$

* Getting the answer quickly: Starting from 2, write down the prime factors of each number, skipping any that don't contribute to the lcm. So we would write 2, then 3. We would skip the prime factors of 6 because 6=2*3 and those have already been written. Then we write 7. So we have 2 3 7. We then multiply these numbers together to get 2*3*7 = 42, choice (D).

Definitions: Recall that {...,-4, -3, -2, -1, 0 , 1, 2, 3, 4,...} form the set of **integers**.

The **positive integers** consist of the positive numbers from that set:

$$\{1, 2, 3, 4,...\}$$

An integer n is **divisible** by an integer d if there is another integer k such that n = dk. For example, 42 is divisible by 7 because 42 = 7*6. In practice we can check if n is divisible by d simply by dividing n by d in our calculator. If the answer is an integer, then n is divisible by d. If the answer is not an integer (it contains digits after the decimal point), then n is not divisible by d.

LEVEL 4: NUMBER THEORY

8. If the product of five consecutive integers written in increasing order equals the middle integer, what is the greatest of the five integers?

    (A) -3
    (B) -2
    (C) 0
    (D) 2
    (E) 3

* Begin by looking at choice (E) since it is the largest. If the greatest integer is 3, then the five consecutive integers are -1, 0, 1, 2, 3 and the product is (-1)*0*1*2*3 = 0. So choice (E) is incorrect, but we can see that if we shift 0 to the middle, then the condition will be satisfied.

$$(-2)(-1)*0*1*2 = 0.$$

The greatest of the five integers is then 2, choice (D).

Caution: A common mistake in this problem is to pick 0 (choice (C)) as the answer. If you're not careful you might forget that the question is asking for the **greatest** of the five integers.

It's not a bad idea to underline the clause "what is the greatest of the five integers?" prior to solving the problem. This type of error occurs so often that it's worth taking some extra precautions.

Note: There is no real computational advantage here in starting with choice (E), but there is a psychological one. By starting with the greatest value, your mind has consciously registered the word "greatest" and you are less likely to fall into the trap of choosing 0 as mentioned above.

A remark about difficulty: Since this is a level 4 problem it is considered somewhat hard. This means that many students got it wrong on an experimental section of the SAT. and so we may be able to eliminate certain choices with about 95% certainty. I call this process **quasi-elimination.** In this problem we could quasi-eliminate choices (A), (C) and (E). Let me explain. If the word greatest appears in a hard problem we can always quasi-eliminate both the largest and smallest value because many students tend to choose one of these when they don't know how to do the problem. We also quasi-eliminate (C) because the word "middle" appears in the problem and choice (C) is the middle answer choice. The topic of quasi-elimination will be covered in more detail below. Note that quasi-elimination only works in **hard** problems (Level 4 or 5).

Definitions: The **integers** are the counting numbers together with their negatives.

$$\{...,-4, -3, -2, -1, 0, 1, 2, 3, 4,...\}$$

Consecutive integers are integers that follow each other in order. The difference between consecutive integers is 1. Here are two examples.

1, 2, 3	these are three consecutive integers
-3, -2, -1, 0, 1	these are five consecutive integers

In general, if x is an integer, then x, x + 1, x +2, x + 3, ... are consecutive integers.

STRATEGY 3
TAKE A GUESS

Sometimes the answer choices themselves cannot be substituted in for the unknown or unknowns in the problem. But that doesn't mean you can't guess your own numbers. Try to make as reasonable a guess as possible, but don't over think it. Keep trying until you zero in on the correct value.

LEVEL 1: GEOMETRY

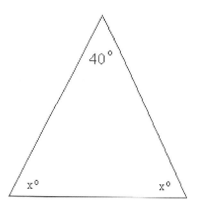

9.   In the triangle above, what is the value of x ?

Recall that a triangle has 180 degrees. We take a guess for x, let's say that x = 60, so the sum of the angles is x + x + 40 = 60 + 60 + 40 = 160 degrees, a bit too small. Let's now try x = 70. Then the sum of the angles is x + x + 40 = 70 + 70 + 40 = 180 degrees. Thus, the answer is **70**.

An algebraic solution: There are 180 degrees in a triangle, so we solve the following equation.

$$x + x + 40 = 180$$
$$2x + 40 = 180$$
$$2x = 140$$
$$x = \mathbf{70}$$

* Mental math: 180 − 40 = 140. Divide 140 by 2 to get x = **70**.

LEVEL 1: ALGEBRA

10. If $k > 0$, for what value of k will $k^2 + 3 = 28$?

Let's take a guess for k, say k = 4. Then k^2 + 3 = 4^2 + 3 = 16 + 3 = 19. This is too small. So let's try a larger value for k, say k = 5. Then

$$k^2 + 3 = 5^2 + 3 = 25 + 3 = 28.$$

Thus, the answer is **5**.

An algebraic solution:

$$k^2 + 3 = 28$$
$$k^2 = 25$$
$$k = \mathbf{5}$$

Remark: The equation k^2 = 25 has two solutions: k = 5 and k = -5. In this question we are given that k > 0, so we reject the negative solution. In easy problems (Level 1 and Level 2), it is pretty safe to reject the negative solution (or not even think about it), but in medium and hard problems (Levels 3, 4 and 5) you need to be more careful.

* Mental math: 28 − 3 = 25. So k = **5**.

LEVEL 3: ALGEBRA

11. If 7 less than x is 2 more than 5, what is the value of x ?

* 2 more than 5 is 5 + 2 = 7. So 7 less than x is 7. Well 7 less than 14 is 7. So x = **14.**

Algebraic solution: "a more than b" means b + a. "a less than b" means b – a. The word "is" means =. So we have

$$x - 7 = 5 + 2$$
$$x - 7 = 7$$
$$x = 14$$

Remark: 5 + 2 = 2 + 5, so technically 2 more than 5 can also be written as 2 + 5 since it gives the same answer. You have to be more careful with "less than" because x – 7 is not the same as 7 – x. So just remember in the expression "a less than b," the numbers reverse positions when we write the algebraic equivalent.

You should also get in the habit of reversing the positions in "a more than b" the same way. In this way you will probably not make a mistake when a problem with the words "less than" comes up.

LEVEL 3: NUMBER THEORY

12. Tom has dogs, cats and birds for pets. The number of birds he has is three times the number of cats, and the number of cats he has is 2 more than the number of dogs. Which of the following could be the total number of these pets?

    (A) 14
    (B) 15
    (C) 16
    (D) 17
    (E) 18

* Let's take a guess and say that Tom has 3 dogs. Then he has 3 + 2 = 5 cats, and 3*5 = 15 birds. So the total number of pets is 3 + 5 + 15 = 23. This is too big. So let's guess that Tom has less dogs, say 1. Then he has 1 + 2 = 3 cats, and 3*3 = 9 birds. So the total is 1 + 3 + 9 = 13. This is too small. So Tom must have 2 dogs, 2 + 2 = 4 cats, and 3*4 = 12 birds for a total of 2 + 4 + 12 = 18 pets. Thus, the answer is choice (E).

Note: We were pretty unlucky to have to take 3 guesses before getting the answer, but even so not too much time was used.

Remark: Attempting to do this algebraically is tedious, time consuming and, for most students, frustrating. The method of "guessing" is much better.

For the advanced student: Although writing out the algebra is not recommended during the SAT, the more advanced student might want to see it done anyway. If we let x represent the number of dogs, then the number of cats is x + 2, and the number of birds is 3(x + 2). Thus, the total number of pets is

$$x + (x + 2) + 3(x + 2) = x + x + 2 + 3x + 6 = 5x + 8.$$

So some possible totals are 13, 18, 23, ... which we get by substituting 1, 2, 3, ... for x.

LEVEL 3: ALGEBRA

13. What is one possible value of x for which $x < 5 < \dfrac{1}{x}$?

* Let's try to guess what x is. Here are some guesses using our calculator to get 1/x as a decimal.

x	1/x
4	.25
2	.5
1	1
.5	2
.1	10

We see that .1 < 5 < 10. So we can grid in **.1**.

Note: When using the symbols < and >, the symbol always points to the smaller number.

Choosing Guesses: If guesses of a certain kind aren't working, try a number of a different kind. For example, in this problem positive integers weren't working, so we switched to decimals less than 1. In general, trying extreme cases is always good. In this case a large integer and a small decimal would get the answer quickly.

In other examples, extreme cases might consist of a positive integer, a negative integer, a positive fraction and a negative fraction. Note that attempting negative numbers would be a waste of time in this problem since we can't grid in a negative number.

An algebraic solution for the advanced student: If 5 < 1/x, then we have 1/5 > x, or equivalently, x < 1/5, or as a decimal x< .2. So we can grid in any answer strictly between 0 and .2. Note that an answer of .2 will be marked wrong (and 0 will be marked wrong as well).

LEVEL 3: ALGEBRA

14. If $3^x = 11$, then $3^{2x} =$

    (A) 5.5
    (B) 22
    (C) 33
    (D) 121
    (E) 1331

Let's try to guess what x is. 3^2 = 9, and 3^3 = 27. So x is between 2 and 3. Now, 3^{2*2} = 3^4 = 81 and 3^{2*3} = 3^6 = 729. Therefore the answer is between 81 and 729. Thus, the answer must be choice (D).

* An algebraic solution for the advanced student: $3^{2x} = (3^x)^2 = 11^2 = 121$. Thus, the answer is choice (D).

If you have forgotten the basic laws of exponents, see p. 57 for a review.

LEVEL 3: GEOMETRY

15. What is the area of a right triangle whose perimeter is 24 and whose sides are z, $z+2$ and $z+4$?

    (A) 6
    (B) 10
    (C) 24
    (D) 48
    (E) 72

Let's try to take a guess for z, say z = 5. Then z + 2 = 7 and z + 4 = 9. Recall that to get the perimeter of a triangle we add up the lengths of all 3 sides. Thus, the perimeter is 5 + 7 + 9 = 21 which is a bit too small. So let's try z = 6, so that we have z + 2 = 8 and z + 4 = 10. Then the perimeter is 6 + 8 + 10 = 24. This is correct, so we have found that z = 6. Therefore the two legs of the triangle have lengths 6 and 8, and the hypotenuse has length 10 (the hypotenuse is always the longest side of a right triangle). In a right triangle we can take the legs to be the base and the height because they are perpendicular. The area of the triangle is therefore

$$A = ½\,b*h = ½\,6*8 = ½\,48 = 24, \text{ choice (C).}$$

* Remark: We can find z algebraically by solving the equation

$$z + (z + 2) + (z + 4) = 24$$
$$3z + 6 = 24$$
$$3z = 18$$
$$z = 6$$

We can then take 6 to be the base and 8 the height as before to get that the area is 24.

STRATEGY 4
PICK A NUMBER

A problem may become much easier to understand and to solve by substituting a specific number in for a variable. Just make sure that you choose a number that satisfies the given conditions.

Here are some guidelines when picking numbers.

(1) Pick a number that's simple but not too simple. In general you might want to avoid picking 0 or 1 (but 2 is usually a good choice).

(2) Try to avoid picking numbers that appear in the problem.

(3) When picking two or more numbers try to make them all different.

(4) Most of the time picking numbers only allows you to eliminate answer choices. So don't just choose the first answer choice that comes out to the correct answer. If multiple answers come out correct you need to pick a new number and start again. But you only have to check the answer choices that haven't yet been eliminated.

(5) If there are fractions in the question a good choice might be the least common denominator (lcd) or a multiple of the lcd.

(6) In percent problems choose the number 100.

(7) Don't pick a negative number as a possible answer to a grid-in question. This is a waste of time since you can't grid a negative number.

(8) If your first attempt doesn't eliminate 4 of the 5 choices, try to choose a number that's of a different "type." Here are some examples of types:

    (a) A positive integer greater than 1.

(b) A positive fraction (or decimal) between 0 and 1.

(c) A negative integer less than -1.

(d) A negative fraction (or decimal) between -1 and 0.

(9) If you're picking pairs of numbers try different combinations from (8). For example you can try two positive integers greater than 1, two negative integers less than -1, or one positive and one negative integer, etc.

Remember that these are just guidelines and there may be rare occasions where you might break these rules. For example sometimes it's so quick and easy to plug in 0 and/or 1 that you might do this even though only some of the answer choices get eliminated.

LEVEL 4: NUMBER THEORY

16. If k is divided by 8, the remainder is 5. What is the remainder if $3k$ is divided by 8?

    (A) 3
    (B) 4
    (C) 5
    (D) 6
    (E) 7

Let's choose a positive integer whose remainder is 5 when it's divided by 8. A simple way to find such a k is to add 8 and 5. So let k = 13. Then we have 3k = 3*13 = 39. 8 goes into 39 four times with a remainder of 7. So, the answer is choice (E).

Important: To find a remainder you must perform division **by hand.** Dividing in your calculator does **not** give you a remainder!

* Note: A slightly simpler choice for k is k = 5. Indeed, when 5 is divided by 8 we get 0 with 5 left over. Then 3k = 15, and the remainder when 15 is divided by 8 is 7, choice (E).

Note that in general we can get a value for k by starting with any multiple of 8 and adding 5. So k = 8n + 5 for some integer n.

Remark: The answer to this problem is independent of our choice for k (assuming that k satisfies the given condition, of course). The method just described does **not** show this. That is not our concern however.

For the advanced student: Here is a complete algebraic solution that actually demonstrates the independence of choice for k. The given condition means that we can write k as $k = 8n + 5$ for some integer n. Then

$$3k = 3(8n + 5) = 24n + 15 = 24n + 8 + 7 = 8(3n + 1) + 7 = 8z + 7$$

where z is the integer $3n + 1$. This shows that when 3k is divided by 8 the remainder is 7, choice (E).

Calculator Algorithm for computing a remainder: Although performing division in your calculator never produces a remainder, there is a simple algorithm you can perform which mimics long division. Let's find the remainder when 39 is divided by 8 using this algorithm.

Step 1: Perform the division in your calculator: $39/8 = 4.875$
Step 2: Multiply the integer part of this answer by the divisor: $4*8 = 32$
Step 3: Subtract this result from the dividend to get the remainder:

$$39 - 32 = \mathbf{7}.$$

Note that in the previous problem the answer choices were numbers (there were no variables). Thus any choice for the variable satisfying the given conditions will lead to the correct answer. If one or more variables appears in the answer choices, we must be more careful.

LEVEL 1: ALGEBRA

17. Which of the following expressions is equivalent to 5 less than the product of x and y ?

  (A) $x + y - 5$
  (B) $xy - 5$
  (C) $5xy$
  (D) $5(x + y)$
  (E) $(x - 5)y$

Let's choose values for x and y, say x = 2, y = 7. Then the product of x and y is 2*7 = 14. So 5 less than the product of x and y is 14 − 5 = **9. Put a nice big, dark circle around this number so that you can find it easily later.** We now substitute 2 for x and 7 for y into each answer choice and use our calculator.

  (A) 2 + 7 − 5 = 4
  (B) 2*7 − 5 = 14 − 5 = 9
  (C) 5*2*7 = 70
  (D) 5(2 + 7) = 5*9 = 45
  (E) (2 − 5)*7 = (-3)*7 = -21

We now compare each of these numbers to the number that we put a nice big, dark circle around. Since (A), (C), (D) and (E) are incorrect we can eliminate them. Therefore the answer is choice (B).

Important note: (B) is **not** the correct answer simply because it is equal to 9. It is correct because all 4 of the other choices are **not** 9. **You absolutely must check all five choices!**

Notice: We didn't use the numbers 0 or 1 because they are so simple that it is more likely for multiple answer choices to come out correct. We would then have to pick new numbers anyway. We also didn't use the number 5 because it appears in the problem. Again, it is more likely that multiple answer choices will come out correct.

* A quick algebraic solution: The product of x and y is xy, and so 5 less than the product of x and y is xy − 5, choice (B).

Common error: A common mistake is to write "5 less than xy" as 5 − xy. This is incorrect. For example, 5 less than 8 is 3. It is **not** -3.

"5 less than 8" = 8 − 5 = 3.
"5 less than the product of x and y" = "5 less than xy" = xy − 5.

LEVEL 3: NUMBER THEORY

18. Which of the following is equal to $\dfrac{k+60}{12}$?

    (A) $\dfrac{k}{12}+5$

    (B) $k+5$

    (C) $5k$

    (D) $\dfrac{k+30}{6}$

    (E) $\dfrac{k+5}{6}$

Let's choose a value for k, say k = 3. We first substitute a 3 in for k into the given expression and use our calculator. We type in the following: (3 + 60)/12 and we get k = **5.25**. **Put a nice big, dark circle around this number so that you can find it easily later.** We now substitute a 3 into each answer choice and use our calculator.

    (A)   3/12 + 5 = 5.25
    (B)   3 + 5 = 8
    (C)   5*3 = 15
    (D)   (3 + 30)/6 = 5.5
    (E)   (3 + 5)/6 ~ 1.33 (~ means "is approximately")

We now compare each of these numbers to the number that we put a nice big, dark circle around. Since (B), (C), (D) and (E) are incorrect we can eliminate them. Therefore the answer is choice (A).

Important note: (A) is **not** the correct answer simply because it is equal to 5.25. It is correct because all 4 of the other choices are **not** 5.25. **You absolutely must check all five choices!**

As an example of how things could go wrong with incorrect reasoning, suppose we choose k = 0. Then the given expression becomes **5**, and the answer choices become

> (A) 5
> (B) 5
> (C) 0
> (D) 5
> (E) 5/6

In this case we have eliminated (C) and (E), but (A), (B) and (D) are **all** potential solutions. A common error is to choose the first answer to come out correct. This is certainly a good guessing strategy, especially if you're running out of time, but it can potentially lead to the wrong answer. This is also why we generally try not to pick numbers to be too simple. It often leads to multiple answer choices coming out to the correct number.

A quick algebraic solution: A discussion of this problem wouldn't be complete without showing how to solve this problem very quickly using an algebraic method.

Most students have no trouble at all adding two fractions with the same denominator. For example,

$$k/12 + 60/12 = (k + 60)/12$$

But these same students have trouble reversing this process.

$$(k + 60)/12 = k/12 + 60/12$$

Note that these two equations are **identical** except that the left and right hand sides have been switched. Note also that to break a fraction into two (or more) pieces, the original denominator is repeated for **each** piece.

* An algebraic solution to the above problem consists of the following quick computation

$$(k + 60)/12 = k/12 + 60/12 = k/12 + 5$$

This is choice (A).

LEVEL 2: ALGEBRA

19. Phil is selling $3d$ DVDs at a price of p dollars each. If x is the number of DVDs he did <u>not</u> sell, which of the following represents the total dollar amount he received in sales from the DVDs?

(A) $px - 3d$
(B) $3d - px$
(C) $3pd - x$
(D) $p(x - 3d)$
(E) $p(3d - x)$

Let's try d = 4, p = 2, x = 5. In this case Phil is selling 12 DVDs at a price of 2 dollars each. He did not sell 5 of them. Thus, he sold 7 of them and therefore he made 7*2 = 14 dollars. **Put a nice big, dark circle around this number so that you can find it easily later.** We now substitute the numbers that we chose into each answer choice.

(A) 2*5 − 3*4 = 10 − 12 = -2
(B) 3*4 − 2*5 = 12 − 10 = 2
(C) 3*2*4 − 5 = 24 − 5 = 19
(D) 2(5 − 3*4) = 2(5 − 12) = 2(-7) = -14
(E) 2(3*4 − 5) = 2(12 − 5) = 2*7 = 14

Since (A), (B), (C) and (D) are incorrect we can eliminate them. Therefore the answer is choice (E).

Important note: (E) is **not** the correct answer simply because it is equal to 14. It is correct because all 4 of the other choices are **not** 14.

Remark: It is not necessary to finish a computation if the answer is clearly incorrect. For example, in choice (D) we could stop at 2(5 − 12) since this is clearly a negative number, and we know that the answer is positive.

* An algebraic solution for the advanced student: Phil sold (3d − x) DVDs (3d is the total and x is the number he did not sell). Thus the total dollar amount Phil received in sales is p(3d − x) (here p is the price per DVD and (3d − x) is the number of DVDs that Phil sold). Thus, the answer is choice (E).

LEVEL 5: ALGEBRA

20. If $a = 3^b$ and $b = c + 4$, what is $\dfrac{a}{27}$ in terms of c ?

    (A) $c + 1$
    (B) 3^c
    (C) 3^{c+1}
    (D) $3^c + 1$
    (E) $3^c + 2$

Let's choose a value for c, say c = 2. Then b = 2 + 4 = 6. So we find a on our calculator as follows: a = 3^6 = 729. Then a/27 = 729/27 = **27. Put a nice big, dark circle around this number so that you can find it easily later.** We now substitute a 2 for c into each answer choice and use our calculator.

    (A) $2 + 1 = 3$
    (B) $3^2 = 9$
    (C) $3^3 = 27$
    (D) $3^2 + 1 = 9 + 1 = 10$
    (E) $3^2 + 2 = 9 + 2 = 11$

We now compare each of these numbers to the number that we put a nice big, dark circle around. Since (A), (B), (D) and (E) are incorrect we can eliminate them. Therefore the answer is choice (C).

Important note: (C) is **not** the correct answer simply because it is equal to 27. It is correct because all four of the other choices are **not** 27. **You absolutely must check all five choices!**

* An algebraic solution for the advanced student: We can solve this problem quickly using algebra.

$$a/27 = 3^b/27 = 3^{c+4}/3^3 = 3^{c+1}.$$

For the last step we subtracted the exponents. We see that the answer is choice (C).

Laws of Exponents: For those students that have forgotten, here is a brief review of the basic laws of exponents.

Law	Example
$x^0 = 1$	$3^0 = 1$
$x^1 = x$	$9^1 = 9$
$x^a x^b = x^{a+b}$	$x^3 x^5 = x^8$
$x^a/x^b = x^{a-b}$	$x^{11}/x^4 = x^7$
$(x^a)^b = x^{ab}$	$(x^5)^3 = x^{15}$
$(xy)^a = x^a y^a$	$(xy)^4 = x^4 y^4$
$(x/y)^a = x^a/y^a$	$(x/y)^6 = x^6/y^6$

LEVEL 5: FUNCTIONS

21. For which of the following functions is it true that $f(-x) = -f(x)$ for all values of x ?

    (A) $f(x) = x^2 + 2$
    (B) $f(x) = x^2 + 2x$
    (C) $f(x) = x^3 + 2x$
    (D) $f(x) = x^3 + 2$
    (E) $f(x) = x + 2$

Let's choose a value for x, say x = 2. We compute f(-2) and -f(2) for each answer choice.

	f(-2)	-f(2)
(A)	6	-6
(B)	0	-8
(C)	-12	-12
(D)	-6	-10
(E)	0	-4

Since choices (A), (B), (D) and (E) don't match up, we can eliminate them. The answer is therefore choice (C).

Note about the notation f(x): The variable x is a placeholder. We evaluate the function f at a specific value by substituting that value in for x. Let's use choice (C) as an example. Here we have

$$f(x) = x^3 + 2x$$
$$f(-2) = (-2)^3 + 2(-2) = -8 - 4 = -12.$$

The other computations in the above table were evaluated in the same manner.

Important note: (C) is **not** the correct answer simply because both computations gave the same answer. It is correct because all 4 of the other choices did **not** work. **You absolutely must check all five choices!**

Caution: These computations involve lots of minus signs. It is therefore very easy to mess them up, even when using a calculator. This is a great problem to test how careful you are when plugging numbers into your calculator.

Some actual math for the more advanced student: A function f with the property that f(-x) = -f(x) for all x is called an **odd** function.

A function f with the property that f(-x) = f(x) is called an **even** function.

Each function given in the answer choices is called a **polynomial function.** These are functions where each **term** has the form ax^n where a is a real number and n is a positive integer.

* Polynomial functions with only odd powers of x are odd functions. Keep in mind that x is the same as x^1, and so x is an odd power of x. From this observation we can see immediately that answer choice (C) is an odd function and thus satisfies the given definition.

Polynomial functions with only even powers of x are even functions. Keep in mind that a constant c is the same as cx^0, and so c is an even power of x. For example 2 is an even power of x. From this observation we can see that the function in answer choice (A) is an even function.

The functions in answer choices (B), (D) and (E) have both even and odd powers of x. They are therefore functions which are neither even nor odd.

A quick graphical analysis of even and odd functions: The graph of an odd function is **symmetrical with respect to the origin**. This means that if you rotate the graph 180 degrees (or equivalently, turn it upside down) it will look the same as it did right side up. If you put choice (C) into your graphing calculator, you will see that this graph has this property.

Similarly, the graph of an even function is **symmetrical with respect to the y-axis**. This means that the y-axis acts like a "mirror," and the graph "reflects" across this mirror. If you put choice (A) into your graphing calculator, you will see that this graph has this property.

Put the other three answer choices in your graphing calculator and observe that they have neither of these symmetries.

So another way to determine if f(-x) = -f(x) is to graph f in your graphing calculator, and see if it looks the same upside down. And another way to determine if f(-x) = f(x) is to graph f in your graphing calculator, and see if the y-axis acts like a mirror. This technique will work for **all** functions (not just polynomials).

LEVEL 3: ALGEBRA

22. If $(\sqrt{x})^k = 7$, what is the value of $\dfrac{1}{x^k}$?

* The nature of the question implies that every choice of k will lead to the same answer (see remark below for an exception). So choose k = 1. Then we have

$$\sqrt{x} = 7, \text{ so that } x = 7^2 = 49.$$

Then $1/x^k = 1/x =$ **1/49**.

Note: As a decimal, $1/49 \sim 0.0204081633$. So we can also grid in **.020**.

Exception: We cannot choose k = 0 because the left side would then become 1 making the given equation 1 = 7 which is false.

An algebraic solution for the advanced student: $(\sqrt{x})^k = x^{k/2}$, so that the equation is $x^{k/2} = 7$. We square both sides to get $x^k = 49$. So $1/x^k =$ **1/49**.

Negative and Fractional Exponents: For those students that have forgotten, here is a brief review of the definitions of fractional and negative exponents.

Law	Example
$x^{-1} = 1/x$	$3^{-1} = 1/3$
$x^{-a} = 1/x^a$	$9^{-2} = 1/81$
$x^{1/n} = \sqrt[n]{x}$	$x^{1/3} = \sqrt[3]{x}$
$x^{m/n} = \sqrt[n]{x^m} = (\sqrt[n]{x})^m$	$x^{9/2} = \sqrt{x^9} = (\sqrt{x})^9$

LEVEL 4: NUMBER THEORY

23. Set A consists of k integers, and the difference between the greatest integer in A and the least integer in A is 725. A new set of k integers, set B, is formed by multiplying each integer in A by 3 and then adding 6 to the product. What is the difference between the greatest integer in B and the least integer in B?

* The question implies that any choice for k will produce the same answer. So, let's choose k = 2, and let A = {0, 725}. Then B = {6, 2181}, and the difference between the greatest and least integer in B is

$$2181 - 6 = \textbf{2175}.$$

An algebraic solution for the advanced student: Let x and y be the least and greatest integers in set A, respectively. Then the least and greatest integers in set B are 3x + 6 and 3y + 6. So the difference between the greatest and least integer in B is

$$(3y + 6) - (3x + 6) = 3y + 6 - 3x - 6 = 3y - 3x = 3(y - x) = 3*725 = \textbf{2175}.$$

Caution: A common mistake is to distribute the minus sign incorrectly. The following computation is **wrong**.

$$(3y + 6) - (3x + 6) = 3y + 6 - 3x + 6$$

LEVEL 3: ALGEBRA

24. If $\dfrac{x}{y} = \dfrac{3}{r}$, which of the following must equal 3?

    (A) x
    (B) y
    (C) r
    (D) $\dfrac{y}{x}$
    (E) $\dfrac{xr}{y}$

Before picking numbers put a nice big, dark circle around the number **3** in the problem. Now let's plug in values for x, y and r. Let's try the following.

$$r = 6 \quad x = 2 \quad y = 4.$$

Notice that we chose the numbers so that they are all distinct, they are all simple but not too simple, and the given equation holds.

Now we substitute these values into each answer choice. Remember that we are looking for the answer to be 3.

    (A) 2
    (B) 4
    (C) 6
    (D) 4/2 = 2
    (E) 2*6/4 = 3

We can eliminate choices (A), (B), (C) and (D) since they did not come out to 3. Thus, the answer is choice (E).

Important note: (E) is **not** the correct answer simply because it is equal to 3. It is correct because all four of the other choices are **not** 3. **You absolutely must check all five choices!**

* **A quick algebraic solution:** Simply multiply both sides of the given equation by r to get 3 by itself. We get xr/y = 3, which is choice (E).

Another option that students seem to like: Many students seem to prefer cross multiplication followed by division so we show this computation here.

$$x/y = 3/r$$
$$xr = 3y$$
$$xr/y = 3.$$

Note that cross multiplying actually creates an additional algebraic step, but the amount of time lost is very small, so it's okay if you prefer this.

LEVEL 5: GEOMETRY

25. On the number line above, point C is the midpoint of $\overline{AB}$. If n is positive, what is the value of k ?

* Since the answer is a number we can choose any positive number for n. Let's take n = 1. Then the 3 numbers from left to right are 3, 3k and 81. So 3k should be the average of 3 and 81.

$$3k = (3 + 81)/2 = 84/2 = 42.$$

Thus k = 42/3 = **14**.

Solution showing the independence of k for the advanced student: $k \cdot 3^n$ should be the average of 3^n and 3^{n+3}. So we have

$k \cdot 3^n = (3^n + 3^{n+3})/2 = (3^n + 3^n 3^3)/2 = 3^n(1 + 27)/2 = 28*3^n/2 = 14 \cdot 3^n$. Thus, we have k = **14**.

Laws of Exponents: For those students that have forgotten, here is a brief review of the basic laws of exponents.

Law	Example
$x^0 = 1$	$3^0 = 1$
$x^1 = x$	$9^1 = 9$
$x^a x^b = x^{a+b}$	$x^3 x^5 = x^8$
$x^a / x^b = x^{a-b}$	$x^{11} / x^4 = x^7$
$(x^a)^b = x^{ab}$	$(x^5)^3 = x^{15}$
$(xy)^a = x^a y^a$	$(xy)^4 = x^4 y^4$
$(x/y)^a = x^a / y^a$	$(x/y)^6 = x^6 / y^6$

LEVEL 5: FUNCTIONS

26. Let the function q be defined by $q(x) = a(x - h)^2$, where h is a positive constant, and a is a negative constant. For what value of x will the function q have its maximum value?

  (A) $-h$
  (B) $-a$
  (C) 0
  (D) a
  (E) h

Let's substitute h = 1 and a = -1, so that q(x) = -(x – 1)². If we put this in our graphing calculator we see that the maximum occurs when x = **1**. Substituting our chosen values for h and a into each answer choice yields

  (A) -1
  (B) 1
  (C) 0
  (D) -1
  (E) 1

We can therefore eliminate choices (A), (C) and (D). Let's try changing h to 2, and leaving a = -1, so that $q(x) = -(x – 2)^2$. Again checking this in our graphing calculator we get x = **2**. Substituting the new values for h and a into answer choices (B) and (E) yields

(B) 1
(E) 2

Choice (B) does not give the correct answer this time so we can eliminate it. Thus, the answer is choice (E).

Remark: If we were a bit more careful about how we picked our original numbers we could have avoided having to do it twice. It is actually easy to see that choosing h = 1 and a = -1 will make some of the answer choices come out to the same number.

Finding the maximum without a graphing calculator: Let's use our second guess (since it turned out to be better).

Method 1: The **standard form** for a quadratic equation is

$$y – k = a(x – h)^2 \text{ or equivalently } y = a(x – h)^2 + k$$

The graph is a parabola with vertex at (h, k). The parabola opens upwards if a > 0, and downwards if a < 0.

$q(x) = -(x – 2)^2$ is the standard form for a quadratic function whose graph is a parabola that opens downwards and has vertex (2, 0). Thus the maximum occurs at x = 2.

Note: In this problem, h = 2 and k = 0. We substituted these values into the standard form for a quadratic equation (either version) and we got $q(x) = -(x – 2)^2$.

Method 2: The **general form** for a quadratic equation is

$$y = ax^2 + bx + c$$

The graph is a parabola whose vertex has x-coordinate –b/2a. The parabola opens upwards if a > 0, and downwards if a < 0.

$q(x)$ = -(x – 2)^2 = -(x^2 – 4x + 4) = -x^2 + 4x – 4. So –b/2a = -4/2(-1) = 2. Thus the maximum occurs at x = 2 (it's a maximum because the parabola opens downwards).

Method 3: For those who know calculus we can use a derivative. The derivative of q(x) = -(x – 2)^2 is q'(x) = -2(x – 2). This is zero when x = 2. The derivative is positive for x < 2 and negative for x > 2 which means that the function is increasing for x < 2 and decreasing for x > 2. Thus, there is a maximum (both relative and absolute) at x = 2.

Note: Any of these last 3 methods can be used from the original equation (without picking numbers). For example, using the first method we have that

* q(x) = a(x – h)^2 is in standard form and thus has a graph that is a parabola with (h, 0) for its vertex. Since a < 0 the parabola opens downwards. Thus the maximum occurs at x = h, choice (E).

LEVEL 2: GEOMETRY

27. In the figure above, the length of AB is $x+5$, the length of BC is $3x-7$ and the length of AD is $4x+4$. What is the length of CD?

    (A) $x+3$
    (B) $x+6$
    (C) 3
    (D) 5
    (E) 6

Let's choose a value for x, say x = 4 (note that we avoid choosing x = 3 since this will make two of the answer choices the same number). Then AB has length 4 + 5 = 9, BC has length 3*4 – 7 = 12 – 7 = 5, and AD has length 4*4 + 4 = 16 + 4 = 20. So CD has length 20 – 9 – 5 = **6. Remember to put a big, dark circle around 6.** Substituting x = 4 into the answer choices gives us the following.

(A) 7
(B) 10
(C) 3
(D) 5
(E) 6

Since (A), (B), (C) and (D) are incorrect we can eliminate them. Therefore the answer is choice (E).

Important note: (E) is **not** the correct answer simply because it is equal to 6. It is correct because all 4 of the other choices are **not** 6.

* A quick algebraic solution:

$$(4x + 4) - (x + 5) - (3x - 7) = 4x + 4 - x - 5 - 3x + 7 = 6.$$

Thus, the answer is choice (E).

A **common error** is to distribute the minus sign incorrectly. Notice that

$$-(x + 5) = -x - 5.$$

It would be incorrect to put a plus sign before the 5 on the right.

If the word percent appears in a problem then the number 100 is an excellent choice for a variable that represents a total. It makes the problem easier than any other choice.

LEVEL 5: PERCENTS

28. There are b bricks that need to be stacked. After k of them have been stacked, then in terms of b and k, what percent of the bricks have not yet been stacked?

(A) $\dfrac{b}{100(b-k)}\%$

(B) $\dfrac{100(b-k)}{b}\%$

(C) $\dfrac{100b}{k}\%$

(D) $\dfrac{100k}{b}\%$

(E) $\dfrac{b}{100k}\%$

Since this is a percent problem we choose 100 for the total number of bricks. So b = 100. For k, let's choose 25, so that 25 bricks have been stacked, and 100 – 25 = 75 have not been stacked. Since we started with 100 as our total, **75%** of the bricks have not been stacked. **Remember to put a big, dark circle around 75%.** We make the substitutions b = 100 and k = 25 into each answer choice.

(A) 100/7500 ~ 0.0133% (~ means "is approximately")
(B) 7500/100 = 75%
(C) 10,000/25 = 400%
(D) 2500/100 = 25%
(E) 25/10,000 = 0.0025%

We now compare each of these percents to the percent that we put a nice big, dark circle around. Since (A), (C), (D) and (E) are incorrect we can eliminate them. Therefore the answer is choice (B).

Important note: (B) is **not** the correct answer simply because it is equal to 75%. It is correct because all 4 of the other choices are **not** 75%. **You absolutely must check all five choices!**

* An algebraic solution for the advanced student: The total number of bricks is b. Since k bricks have been stacked, it follows that b − k have not been stacked. To get the **fraction** of bricks that have not been stacked we divide the **number** that have not been stacked by the total. This is (b − k)/b. To change this to a **percent** we multiply by 100, to get 100(b − k)/b %.

Note: The last step in the algebraic solution is equivalent to the usual ratio computation where we are changing the denominator to 100.

$$
\begin{array}{lll}
\text{bricks not stacked} & b - k & x \\
\text{total bricks} & b & 100
\end{array}
$$

$$(b - k)/b = x/100$$
$$100(b - k) = bx$$
$$100(b - k)/b = x$$

See the strategy "Setting up a ratio" below for a more detailed explanation.

In percent problems it sometimes pays to choose the number 100 even though the problem doesn't indicate that you need to choose anything.

LEVEL 5: PERCENTS

29. If Matt's weight increased by 30 percent and Lisa's weight decreased by 20 percent during a certain year, the ratio of Matt's weight to Lisa's weight at the end of the year was how many times the ratio at the beginning of the year?

* Since this is a percent problem, let's choose 100 pounds for both Matt's weight and Lisa's weight at the beginning of the year. Matt's weight at the end of the year was then 100 + 30 = 130 pounds and Lisa's weight at the end of the year was 100 − 20 = 80 pounds. We then have that the ratio of Matt's weight to Lisa's weight at the beginning of the year was 100/100 = 1, and the ratio of Matt's weight to Lisa's weight at the end of the year was 130/80 = 13/8. We can therefore grid in **13/8**.

Notes:

(1) The computations are only this simple because we chose both numbers to be 100. Let's choose different numbers so that you can see how the computations become more difficult. Let's choose 150 pounds for Matt's weight at the beginning of the year and 75 pounds for Lisa's weight at the beginning of the year. 30% of 150 is 150(.3) = 45. So we have that Matt's weight was 150 + 45 = 195 at the end of the year. Also, 20% of 75 is 75(.2) = 15 pounds. It follows that Lisa's weight at the end of the year was 75 − 15 = 60 pounds. The ratio of Matt's weight to Lisa's weight at the beginning of the year was 150/75 = 2, and the ratio of Matt's weight to Lisa's weight at the end of the year was 195/60 = 3.25. Finally, we have to solve the equation

$$2x = 3.25$$
$$x = 3.25/2 = 1.625 \text{ or } 13/8$$

So we do get the same answer, but we put in a lot more effort.

(2) 13/8 is equal to 1.625 as a decimal. Thus, we can also grid in **1.62** or **1.63**. We get 1.62 by truncating the decimal, and 1.63 by rounding the decimal. Truncating is better because less thought is involved. Note that if you grid in 1.6 the answer will be marked wrong.

For the advanced student: Let's solve this problem directly. Let Matt's and Lisa's weights at the beginning of the year be x and y, respectively. Then at the end of the year their weights are 1.3x and 0.8y. The ratio of Matt's weight to Lisa's weight at the beginning of the year was x/y, and the ratio of Matt's weight to Lisa's weight at the end of the year was 1.3x/0.8y = 13/8 * x/y which is 13/8 times the ratio at the beginning of the year. We can therefore grid in **13/8**.

STRATEGY 5

PLUG IN THE
GIVEN POINTS

*J*f the graph of a function or other equation passes through certain points, plug those points into the equation to eliminate answer choices.

LEVEL 3: GEOMETRY

30. Which of the following is an equation of the line in the xy-plane that passes through the point $(0,-5)$ and is perpendicular to the line $y = -3x + 6$?

    (A) $y = -3x + 5$

    (B) $y = -3x + 10$

    (C) $y = -\dfrac{1}{3}x + 6$

    (D) $y = \dfrac{1}{3}x - 5$

    (E) $y = \dfrac{1}{3}x + 5$

* Since the point (0, -5) lies on the line, if we substitute 0 in for x, we should get -5 for y. Let's substitute 0 in for x in each answer choice.

(A) 5
(B) 10
(C) 6
(D) -5
(E) 5

We can eliminate choices (A), (B), (C) and (E) because they did not come out to -5. The answer is therefore choice (D).

Important note: (D) is **not** the correct answer simply because y came out to -5. It is correct because all 4 of the other choices did **not** give -5 for y.

An algebraic solution for the advanced student: Recall the slope-intercept form for the equation of a line.

$$y = mx + b$$

(0, -5) is the y-intercept of the point. Thus, b = -5. The slope of the given line is -3. Since the new line is perpendicular to this line, its slope is the **negative reciprocal** of -3, which is 1/3. So m = 1/3 and the equation of the new line is

$$y = 1/3\ x - 5.$$

Thus, the answer is choice (D).

Note: To get the reciprocal of a number we interchange the numerator and denominator. The number -3 has a "hidden" denominator of 1, so the reciprocal of -3 is -1/3. Now to get the negative reciprocal, we simply change the sign of the reciprocal. Thus, the negative reciprocal of -3 is 1/3.

Recall: Parallel lines have the same slope, and perpendicular lines have slopes that are negative reciprocals of each other.

LEVEL 4: FUNCTIONS

x	-2	0	2
$f(x)$	$\dfrac{3}{25}$	3	75

31. The table above shows some values for the function f. If $f(x) = ab^x$ for some positive constants a and b, what is the value of b?

* Let's start with the easiest point (0, 3). Equivalently, 3 = f(0) = ab^0 = a.

So the function is now f(x) = $3b^x$. Let's use the point (2, 75) to find b. Equivalently, 75 = f(2) = $3b^2$ so that b^2 = 25 and b = **5** (since b is positive).

Thus, the answer is **5**.

Notes: (1) b^2 = 25 actually has the two solutions b = 5 and b = -5. We reject the negative solution in this problem because it is specifically mentioned that b is a positive constant.

   (2) Be careful with order of operations here. Exponentiation is always done before multiplication. So ab^x means raise b to the x power, and **then** multiply by a. **Do not** multiply a times b first.

Order of Operations: A quick review of order of operations.

PEMDAS	
P	Parentheses
E	Exponentiation
M	Multiplication
D	Division
A	Addition
S	Subtraction

Note that multiplication and division have the same priority, and addition and subtraction have the same priority.

STRATEGY 6
FIGURES ARE DRAWN TO SCALE
UNLESS STATED OTHERWISE

*Y*ou may assume that a figure **is** drawn to scale unless it specifically says it is not.

LEVEL 1: GEOMETRY

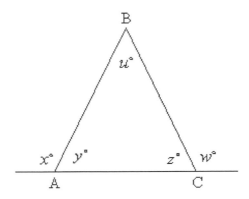

32. In $\triangle ABC$ above, $AB = BC$. Which of the following must be true?

   (A) $u = y$
   (B) $u = z$
   (C) $u = x$
   (D) $u = w$
   (E) $x = w$

* We can assume that the figure is drawn to scale. Clearly u is less than 90 and x and w are greater than 90, so we can eliminate choices (C) and (D). It seems like y and z are both larger than u as well, so choices (A) and (B) can be eliminated. It looks like x = w, so the answer is choice (E).

Some geometry: Since AB = BC, the two angles opposite these sides are congruent. Thus, y = z. Then x = 180 − y = 180 − z = w. So the answer is choice (E).

LEVEL 3: GEOMETRY

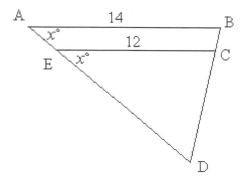

33. In the figure above, what is the value of $\dfrac{ED}{AD}$?

(A) $\dfrac{1}{7}$

(B) $\dfrac{1}{4}$

(C) $\dfrac{2}{5}$

(D) $\dfrac{1}{2}$

(E) $\dfrac{6}{7}$

* Clearly ED is more than half the size of AD, so that ED/AD > 1/2. Thus, the answer is 6/7, choice (E).

Some geometry: Triangles ECD and ABD are **similar**, and corresponding sides of similar triangles are in proportion. Therefore,

$$ED/AD = EC/AB = 12/14 = 6/7$$

Thus, the answer is choice (E).

Definition of similar: Two triangles are **similar** if their angles are congruent.

Note that similar triangles **do not** have to be the same size.

Also note that to show that that two triangles are similar we need only show that two pairs of angles are congruent. We get the third pair for free because all triangles have 180 degrees.

In this problem we have that angles BAD and CED are congruent, and the two triangles share angle D.

LEVEL 1: GEOMETRY

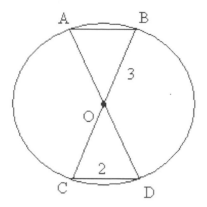

34. In the figure above, if O is the center of the circle, and AD and BC are diameters, which of the following statements is true?

(A) $OC > 3$
(B) $AB > 2$
(C) $AB = 2$
(D) $OA = 2$
(E) $OA < 2$

* We can assume that the figure is drawn to scale. It looks like AB and CD have the same length. So AB = 2 and the answer is choice (C).

Remark: It also looks like OA = OB = OC = OD, but there is no answer choice saying that any of these are equal to 3.

Some geometry: Since OA, OB, OC and OD are all radii of the circle, they are equal in length. Thus OA = OB = OC = OD = 3. The angles AOB and COD are **vertical angles** and are thus congruent. Minor arcs AB and CD have the same measure as angles AOB and COD, respectively since these two angles are central angles (**central angles have the same degree measure as their intercepted arcs**). Thus minor arcs AB and CD have the same measure. **If two minor arcs are equal in measure, their corresponding chords are equal in measure**. Therefore AB = CD = 2.

STRATEGY 7
WHEN FIGURES AREN'T DRAWN TO SCALE

*H*ere are some things we can do when a figure is not drawn to scale.

1. **Do nothing**. Sometimes the exact dimensions of the figure are not important to solving the problem. In this case just use the given information to get the answer.

2. **Redraw the figure to scale.** Redrawing the figure using the given information may make the problem easier to solve.

3. **Draw two or more distinct representations of the figure.** Sometimes the given information leaves open two or more possibilities for how the figure can look. Usually two distinct representations will do the trick (the one that is given and one more). Try to make the representations as different as possible.

LEVEL 5: GEOMETRY

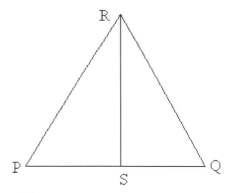

Note: Figure not drawn to scale.

35. In $\triangle PRQ$ above, $PS = SQ$. Which of the following must be true?

   (A) Area of $\triangle PRS$ = area of $\triangle QRS$
   (B) Perimeter of $\triangle PRS$ = perimeter of $\triangle QRS$
   (C) Measure of $\angle RPS$ = measure of $\angle RQS$
   (D) Measure of $\angle RSP$ = measure of $\angle RSQ$
   (E) $PR = RQ$

We begin by drawing another representation of the figure that is very different from this one (but consistent with the given information of course).

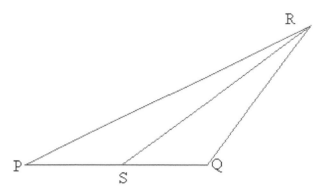

Just by looking at this new figure we can immediately eliminate choices (C), (D) and (E). Since PR > RQ in this new figure, PS = SQ, and both triangles share the side SR, we see that we can also eliminate choice (B). Thus, by process of elimination the answer is choice (A).

* A solution without drawing a second figure: The area of a triangle is given by the formula A = ½ bh. Both triangles have equal bases because PS = SQ. Recall that the height of a triangle is the perpendicular distance from the vertex not on the base to the line containing the base. In the original figure that distance is probably BC (whether the picture is accurate is irrelevant – the point is that the height is the same). Therefore both triangles also have equal heights. Since the two triangles have the same base and the same height, they have the same area. So the answer is choice (A).

Remark: Although this is not necessary to solve this particular problem, it is worth observing what the height is for the triangle directly above. It is labeled with an h in the following picture.

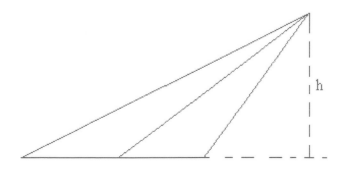

80

STRATEGY 8
EXAGGERATE THE SITUATION

Sometimes you may want to draw or redraw a picture exaggerating the given information. For example, if it is stated that one side is longer than another, draw the longer side **really** long and the shorter side **really** short. Same thing goes for angles.

LEVEL 3: GEOMETRY

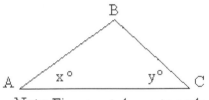

Note: Figure not drawn to scale.

36. In $\triangle ABC$ above, if $x < y$, which of the following must be true?

   (A) $AB < BC$
   (B) $AB < AC$
   (C) $AB = BC$
   (D) $AB > BC$
   (E) $AB > AC$

We redraw the figure with the situation exaggerated. We make x very small and y very big.

From this picture we can eliminate choices (A), (B) and (C). If we were stuck here, we would take a guess between (D) and (E).

Let's finish the problem. Look back at the original figure. In that figure y is just a little bigger than x, and we see that we can eliminate answer choice (E). Thus the answer is choice (D).

* Alternate Solution: Since $x < y$, the side opposite x is shorter than the side opposite y. Thus BC < AB, or equivalently AB > BC, choice (D).

Remark: The alternate solution uses Strategy 26 from this book.

STRATEGY 9
DRAW YOUR
OWN FIGURE

*I*f the problem doesn't have a figure above it, then don't hesitate to draw your own. Sometimes drawing a quick picture of the situation makes the problem very easy, or at least easier. This is especially helpful in geometry problems.

LEVEL 1: GEOMETRY

37. Segment $\overline{PQ}$ has midpoint M. If the length of $\overline{PM}$ is t, what is the length of $\overline{PQ}$ in terms of t?

　　(A) t
　　(B) $2t$
　　(C) $3t$
　　(D) $4t$
　　(E) $5t$

* Let's begin by drawing a picture

From the picture we see that PQ has twice the length of PM. Thus, the length of PQ is 2t, choice (B).

Note: If the variable t still confuses you after drawing the picture, pick a number for t, and substitute that number into the answer choices. For example, we can let t = 2, so that the picture looks as follows.

We see that PQ must be **4.** Substituting 2 for t into each answer choice we get

       (A) 2
       (B) 4
       (C) 6
       (D) 8
       (E) 20

We can therefore eliminate choices (A), (C), (D) and (E). Thus, the answer is choice (B).

LEVEL 2: GEOMETRY

38. What is the area of a right triangle whose sides have lengths 14, 48, and 50?

Let's begin by drawing a picture.

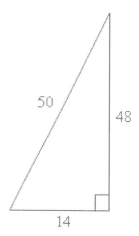

Remember: The **hypotenuse** of a right triangle (the side opposite the right angle) is always longer than both **legs**.

* In a right triangle we can always take the two legs to be the base and the height (in either order). So b = 14, h = 48, and

$$A = \frac{1}{2} b*h = \frac{1}{2} \ 14*48 = \textbf{336}.$$

LEVEL 3: GEOMETRY

39. If line m is perpendicular to segment PQ at point R and $PR = RQ$, how many points on line m are equidistant from point P and point Q?

   (A) One
   (B) Two
   (C) Three
   (D) Four
   (E) More than four

Recall first that **equidistant** means at the same distance. So we're looking for points on line m that are at the same distance from P as they are from Q. Let's begin by drawing a picture:

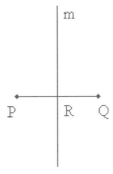

Notice that R is equidistant from P and Q so there is at least one. Let's draw some more.

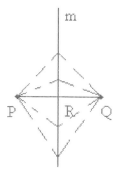

Since there are 5 shown in the above picture, the answer is choice (E).

* **Note:** Every point on line m is actually equidistant from P and Q. m is the **perpendicular bisector** of line segment PQ.

Definition: The **perpendicular bisector** of a line segment is a line perpendicular to the segment that passes through the midpoint of the segment.

LEVEL 4: GEOMETRY

40. Point A is a vertex of a 6-sided polygon. The polygon has 6 sides of equal length and 6 angles of equal measure. When all possible diagonals are drawn from point A in the polygon, how many triangles are formed?

    (A) One
    (B) Two
    (C) Three
    (D) Four
    (E) Six

* We draw a picture.

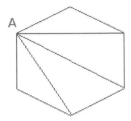

Observe that there are four triangles, choice (D).

LEVEL 5: GEOMETRY

41. In rectangle $PQRS$, point T is the midpoint of side PQ. If the area of quadrilateral $QRST$ is 0.8, what is the area of rectangle $PQRS$?

* Let's begin by drawing a picture.

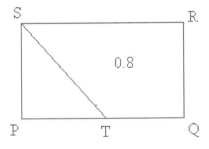

This picture alone really sheds some light on the situation. Lets now chop up our picture into 4 equal parts.

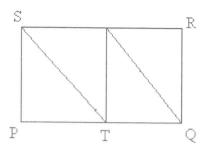

To get the area of one of those pieces simply divide 0.8 by 3. In our calculator we get

.266666666666667 or 4/15 if we change back to a fraction.

This is ¼ of the area of the rectangle, so we simply multiply this result by 4 to get the answer.

We get 1.066666667. So we can grid in **1.06** or **1.07**.

Note: We cannot grid in the answer as a fraction since there are not enough slots in the grid for 16/15.

In some problems we may want to redraw part of a given figure to make the picture easier to understand.

LEVEL 3: GEOMETRY

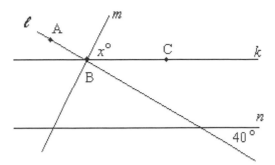

Note: Figure not drawn to scale.

42. In the figure above, line k is parallel to line n. If line m bisects angle ABC , what is the value of x ?

* This is a standard SAT problem involving two parallel lines cut by a transversal. In this example there are actually two transversals. It's useful to isolate just one of them. We do this below.

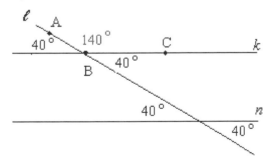

Note: Figure not drawn to scale.

Note that the transversal ℓ creates 8 angles, four of which have measure 40 degrees. The other four are 140 degrees (only one is labeled in the picture). Any two non-congruent angles are supplementary, ie. they add up to 180 degrees. Finally we note that x is half of 140 because line m bisects angle ABC. Thus x = **70**.

STRATEGY 10
QUASI-ELIMINATION
IN HARD PROBLEMS

*T*he experimental section of the SAT is used to determine the difficulty level of an SAT question when it's put on a later exam. If lots of students get a question correct it is considered "easy" and it will appear within the first third of a math section. If the majority of students get a question wrong it is considered "hard" and put in the last third of a section. This method of question placement has a flaw which we can exploit. In some hard questions by taking a moment to think about why most students got the problem wrong we can eliminate some answer choices with 95% certainty. Here are the two main reasons that a student gets a hard problem wrong.

(1) The student simply didn't know how to do the problem, so they took a guess. Either consciously or subconsciously the student may have picked up on a key word in the question and used that information when they decided on a guess.

(2) The student was tricked.

You can quasi-eliminate a choice by crossing it off just like you would if you were eliminating it. Just be aware that there is a tiny chance that it could still be correct.

After quasi-eliminating a choice, you should only choose it as an answer if you can give a complete justification as to why it is correct. If you cannot, then take a guess among the remaining choices.

Remember: Quasi-elimination should only be used for hard problems.

Here are some of the most common times you should use quasi-elimination:

(1) If the word "least" appears in a problem, quasi-eliminate both the smallest and largest answer (generally choices (A) and (E)).

(2) If the word "greatest" appears in a problem, quasi-eliminate both the smallest and largest answer (generally choices (A) and (E)).

(3) If the word "middle" appears in the problem quasi-eliminate choice (C).

(4) If you can add, subtract, multiply or divide two numbers in the problem to get an answer choice, quasi-eliminate that choice.

(5) Always quasi-eliminate the choice "It cannot be determined from the information given."

(6) If your current SAT score is below a 600 and you get an answer very quickly, then quasi-eliminate that choice – you've probably been tricked.

(7) If the answer seems completely obvious, then quasi-eliminate that choice.

Remember: Quasi-elimination should only be used for hard problems.
(This statement is written twice intentionally—it cannot be stressed enough)

Level 4: Number Theory

43. Joseph drove from home to work at an average speed of 30 miles per hour and returned home along the same route at an average speed of 45 miles per hour. If his total driving time for the trip was 3 hours, how many <u>minutes</u> did it take Joseph to drive from work to home?

    (A) 135
    (B) 72
    (C) 60
    (D) 50
    (E) 30

Since 30 appears in the problem we quasi-eliminate choice (E). Since 45*3 = 135 and both 45 and 3 appear in the problem we quasi-eliminate choice (A). Let's also quasi-eliminate choice (C) since the word "minutes" appears and the number 60 is easily associated with this word. If we didn't know how to do the problem, we would take a guess between (B) and (D).

Solution by starting with choice (C): Let's start with choice (C). If it took Joseph 60 minutes (or 1 hour) to get from work to home, then the distance from work to home is d = 45 miles. This is the same as the distance from home to work. Therefore, the total time for Joseph to get from home to work would be t = d/r = 45/30 = 1.5 hours. But that means that the total trip only took 2.5 hours. So we can eliminate choices (C), (D), and (E). Since Joseph is traveling faster from work to home, it should take him less than half the time to get home. So the answer is less than 1.5 hours = 90 minutes. This eliminates choice (A), and therefore the answer is choice (B).

* Solution by estimation: 3 hours is the same as 180 minutes. If John was travelling at the same rate for the whole trip, it would take him exactly half this time to get from work to home, 90 minutes. Since Jon is travelling a little faster on the way from work to home, the answer will be a little less than 90, most likely 72, choice (B).

An algebraic solution: We use the simple formula distance = rate * time. Let's put the given information into the following chart.

	Distance	Rate	Time
home to work	d	30	d/30
work to home	d	45	d/45
total			3

Note that although we don't know either distance, we do know that they are the same, so we can call them both "d."

Also, since distance = rate * time, we have that time = distance/rate. We use this to get the first two entries in column three. The total time is given in the question. So we have

$$d/30 + d/45 = 3$$
$$45d + 30d = 3*30*45$$
$$75d = 3*30*45$$
$$d = 3*30*45/75$$

We want the time it takes Joseph to drive from work to home, that is we want d/45.

This is equal to d/45 = 3*30/75 in hours. To convert to minutes we multiply by 60.

$$d/45 = 3*30*60/75 = 72 \text{ minutes, choice (B)}.$$

A solution using Xiggi's formula (Note: Xiggi's formula is one of the Bonus Strategies at the end of this book. You should read and understand that section before attempting to understand this solution):

Average Speed = 2(30)(45)/(30 + 45) =36
So Total Round Trip Distance = r*t =36*3 = 108
Distance from Work to Home = 108/2 = 54
Time from Work to Home = distance/rate = 54/45 = 1.2.

Finally multiply by 60 to convert to minutes. 1.2*60 = 72, choice (B).

Remark: This example shows that Xiggi's formula does not always immediately give a solution. It depends on what is being asked.

LEVEL 5: NUMBER THEORY

44. Let A be the set of positive factors of 18 and let B be the set of positive factors of 10. If x is a member of the set A and y is a member of the set B, what is the greatest possible value of $x - y$?

   (A) 2
   (B) 8
   (C) 15
   (D) 17
   (E) 18

Since the word **greatest** appears in the problem we quasi-eliminate choices (A) and (E). Since 18 − 10 = 8, we quasi-eliminate choice (B). If we had no idea how to do the problem we would take a guess between choices (C) and (D).

* **Solution:** To make x − y as large as possible, we make x as large as possible, and y as small as possible. The largest positive factor of 18 is 18 (every integer is a factor of itself), so x = 18. The smallest positive factor of 10 is 1 (1 is a factor of every integer), so y = 1. Thus

$$x - y = 18 - 1 = 17, \text{ choice (D)}.$$

Remark: The complete set of positive factors of 18 is {1, 2, 3, 6, 9, 18}. The set of factors of 10 is {1, 2, 5, 10}.

LEVEL 5: GEOMETRY

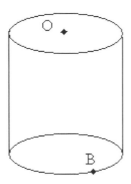

45. The figure above shows a right circular cylinder with diameter 4 and height 7. If point O is the center of the top of the cylinder and B lies on the circumference of the bottom of the cylinder, what is the straight-line distance between O and B ?

    (A) 3
    (B) 7
    (C) 11
    (D) $\sqrt{53}$
    (E) $\sqrt{65}$

Since 7 is in the problem we can quasi-eliminate choice (B). We can also quasi-eliminate choices (A) and (C) because 7 − 4 = 3 and 7 + 4 = 11. So if we didn't know how to do the problem we would take a guess between (D) and (E).

* **Solution:** We draw a right triangle inside the cylinder as follows.

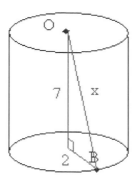

Note that the bottom leg of the triangle is equal to the radius of the circle (not the diameter) which is why it is 2 and not 4. We can now use the Pythagorean Theorem to find x.

$$x^2 = 2^2 + 7^2 = 4 + 49 = 53$$

So x = $\sqrt{53}$, choice (D).

Note: In this case quasi-elimination eliminated 3 incorrect answer choices. Just remember that quasi-elimination is a good guessing strategy, but it is not 100% reliable. It is certainly not a substitute for actually attempting the problem.

Level 4: Functions

46. For all numbers x, define the function h by $h(x) = 2x + 6$. Which of the following is equal to $h(6) + h(5)$?

   (A) $h(11)$
   (B) $h(14)$
   (C) $h(30)$
   (D) $h(32)$
   (E) $h(34)$

We quasi-eliminate choice (A) because 6 + 5 = 11. We quasi-eliminate choice (C) because 6*5 = 30. Now let's compute.

*   h(6) = 2*6 + 6 = 12 + 6 = 18
       h(5) = 2*5 + 6 = 10 + 6 = 16
       h(6) + h(5) = 18 + 16 = 34

Now look carefully – answer choice (E) is **not** 34. It is h(34). The answer is probably choice (B) or (D). So let's start with choice (B) as our first guess.

h(14) = 2*14 + 6 = 28 + 6 = 34. This is correct, so that the answer is choice (B).

Remark: If (B) and (D) did not give the correct value, then we would of course still try (A), (C) and (E). There is a 5% chance that one of these is correct.

LEVEL 5: NUMBER THEORY

47. If k can be any integer such that $7 < \sqrt{k} < 15$, what is the difference between the largest possible value of k and the smallest possible value of k ?

    (A) 4
    (B) 8
    (C) 22
    (D) 174
    (E) 176

We quasi-eliminate (A) and (E) because the word largest (and smallest) appears in the problem. We quasi-eliminate (B) because 15 − 7 = 8. We quasi-eliminate (C) because 15 + 7 = 22. There is therefore a 95% chance that the answer is choice (D). Now let's do the problem.

* Squaring each part of the given inequality gives 49 < k < 225. Thus, the answer is 224 − 50 = 174, choice (D).

98

STRATEGY 11
DIFFERENCES OF
LARGE SUMS

*T*he quickest way to subtract two large sums is to follow these steps:

(1) Write out each sum formally.
(2) Figure out how to line them up properly.
(3) Subtract term by term.
(4) Finish the computation.

This is best understood with examples.

LEVEL 5: NUMBER THEORY

48. If x denotes the sum of the integers from 1 to 50 inclusive, and y denotes the sum of the integers from 51 to 100 inclusive, what is the value of $y - x$?

    (A) 50
    (B) 51
    (C) 500
    (D) 1250
    (E) 2500

We write out each sum formally and line them up with y above x.

$$51 + 52 + 53 + ... + 100$$

$$1 + 2 + 3 + \ldots + 50$$

Now subtract term by term.

$$
\begin{array}{r}
51 + 52 + 53 + \ldots + 100 \\
\underline{1 + 2 + 3 + \ldots + 50} \\
50 + 50 + 50 + \ldots + 50
\end{array}
$$

Now notice that we're adding 50 to itself 50 times. This is the same as multiplying 50 by 50. So we get 50*50 = 2500, choice (E).

Remark: Although it is possible to get the answer by performing these long computations in your calculator, this is not recommended. Most students do not get the correct answer this way due to computational error. Also, a lot of time is wasted.

* Quick computation: Once you get a little practice with this type of problem you can simply compute 50*50 = 2500, choice (E).

Quasi-elimination Note: We can quasi-eliminate choices (A) and (B) since 50 and 51 appear in the problem.

Using the sum feature on your graphing calculator: Here's an alternate solution using your graphing calculator.

Press the **2nd** button followed by the **List** button (same as **Stat** button).
Go to **Math** and select **5: sum(** or press **5**.
Press **2nd** followed by **List** again.
Go to **Ops** and select **5: seq(** or press **5**.
Enter **x, x, 1, 50))**.
The display should look like this:

sum(seq(x, x, 1, 50))

Press **Enter** and you should get the answer **1275**.

Next enter **sum(seq(x, x, 51, 100))** and you should get the answer **3775**. Finally, 3775 − 1275 = 2500, choice (E).

Time Saving Remark: After entering **sum(seq(x, x, 1, 50))** and getting an answer of 1275, you can press the **2nd** button followed by the **Enter** button to bring **sum(seq(x, x, 1, 50))** back up in the calculator. Then move the cursor back, change the 1 to a 51 and the 50 to 100 and press **Enter** again.

Arithmetic series solution (not recommended for the SAT)**:** The sum of the terms of a sequence is called a **series**. A series is **arithmetic** if any two consecutive terms have the same difference. There is a simple formula for the sum of an arithmetic series:

A$_n$ = n*m where **n** is the number of terms and **m** is the average (arithmetic mean) of the first and last term.

The sum of the integers from 1 to 50 inclusive is 50*(1 + 50)/2 = 1275, and the sum from 51 to 100 inclusive is 50*(51 + 100)/2 = 3775. Therefore y – x = 3775 – 1275 = 2500, choice (E).

Exercise for the advanced student: Derive the above formula for the sum of an arithmetic series.

Hint: If a$_1$, a$_2$, ..., a$_n$ are the terms of the series, formally add them both forwards and backwards, and then use the same trick that was applied in the first solution to problem 48.

LEVEL 5: NUMBER THEORY

49. The sum of the positive odd integers less than 150 is subtracted from the sum of the positive even integers less than or equal to 150. What is the resulting difference?

We write out each sum formally and line them up term by term.

$$2 + 4 + 6 + ... + 150$$
$$1 + 3 + 5 + ... + 149$$

Now subtract term by term.

$$2 + 4 + 6 + \ldots + 150$$
$$1 + 3 + 5 + \ldots + 149$$
$$1 + 1 + 1 + \ldots + \quad 1$$

Now notice that we're adding 1 to itself 75 times. So the answer is **75**.

Note: It is easiest to see that we are adding 75 ones by looking at the sum of the positive even integers less than or equal to 150. There are 150/2 = 75 terms in this sum.

* **Quick computation:** Once you get a little practice with this type of problem you can simply compute 75*1 = **75**.

Using the sum feature on your graphing calculator: Here's an alternate solution using your graphing calculator.

Press the **2nd** button followed by the **List** button (same as **Stat** button).
Go to **Math** and select **5: sum(** or press **5**.
Press **2nd** followed by **List** again.
Go to **Ops** and select **5: seq(** or press **5**.
Enter **x, x, 1, 149, 2))**.
The display should look like this:

sum(seq(x, x, 1, 149, 2))

Press **Enter** and you should get the answer **5625.**

Next enter **sum(seq(x, x, 2, 150, 2))** and you should get the answer **5700**. Finally, 5700 − 5625 = **75**.

Note: In the expression **sum(seq(x, x, 2, 150, 2))** the last 2 indicates the **step size**. Here we are adding every other number.

Time Saving Remark: After entering **sum(seq(x, x, 1, 149, 2))** and getting an answer of 1275, you can press the **2nd** button followed by the **Enter** button to bring **sum(seq(x, x, 1, 149, 2))** back up in the calculator. Then move the cursor back, change the 1 to a 2 and the 149 to 150 and press **Enter** again.

Arithmetic series solution (not recommended for the SAT): The formula for the sum of an arithmetic series is, **A$_n$ = n*m** (see page 101). So, the sum of the positive odd integers less than 150 is 75*(1 + 149)/2 = 5625. Also, the sum of the positive even integers less than or equal to 150 is 75*(2 + 150)/2 = 5700. Therefore the difference is 5700 − 5625 = **75**.

LEVEL 5: ALGEBRA

50. Let $x \circ y$ be defined as the sum of all integers between x and y. For example, $1 \circ 4 = 2 + 3 = 5$. What is the value of $(50 \circ 1000) - (52 \circ 999)$?

* We write out each sum formally and line them up so that the numbers match up.

$$51 + 52 + 53 + 54 + \ldots + 998 + 999$$
$$53 + 54 + \ldots + 998$$

Now subtract term by term.

$$51 + 52 + 53 + 54 + \ldots + 998 + 999$$
$$\underline{\quad 53 + 54 + \ldots + 998 \quad}$$
$$51 + 52 + 0 + 0 + \ldots + 0 + 999$$

So the answer is 51 + 52 + 999 = **1102**.

Remark: The advanced student might want to practice doing this computation quickly in their head. A solution using the formula for the sum of an arithmetic series may also be used here, but this is certainly not the quickest method.

LEVEL 5: ALGEBRA

51. Let $\langle x \rangle$ be defined as the sum of the integers from 1 to x, inclusive. Which of the following equals $\langle 21 \rangle - \langle 20 \rangle$?

    (A) $\langle 1 \rangle$
    (B) $\langle 2 \rangle$
    (C) $\langle 5 \rangle$
    (D) $\langle 6 \rangle$
    (E) $\langle 21 \rangle$

We write out each sum formally and line them up with y above x.

$$1 + 2 + 3 + \ldots + 20 + 21$$
$$1 + 2 + 3 + \ldots + 20$$

Now subtract term by term.

$$\begin{array}{r} 1 + 2 + 3 + \ldots + 20 + 21 \\ \underline{1 + 2 + 3 + \ldots + 20 } \\ 0 + 0 + 0 + \ldots + 0 + 21 \end{array}$$

So, we get 21. But 21 is **not** an answer choice. Don't be tricked into choosing choice (E).

We begin with choice (C) and compute <5> = 1 + 2 + 3 + 4 + 5 = 15.

This is too small, so we eliminate choices (A), (B) and (C). Let's check (D).

<6> = 1 + 2 + 3 + 4 + 5 + 6 = 21. Thus, the answer is choice (D).

* Quick computation: <21> − <20> = 21 = 1 + 2 + 3 + 4 + 5 + 6 = <6>.

Quasi-elimination note: We can quasi-eliminate answer choice (A) because 21 − 20 = 1, and 21 and 20 both appear in the question. We can quasi-eliminate (E) since 21 appears in the question.

STRATEGY 12
PERCENT CHANGE

*M*emorize the following very simple formula for percent change problems.

$$Percent\ Change = \frac{Change}{Original} \times 100$$

Note that this is the same formula for both a percent increase or a percent decrease problem.

This formula is **not** given to you on the SAT and **must be memorized.**

LEVEL 2: PERCENTS

52. In January, Jennifer was able to type 28 words per minute. In February she was able to type 35 words per minute. By what percent did Jennifer's speed increase from January to February?

    (A) 7%
    (B) 10%
    (C) 25%
    (D) 28%
    (E) 35%

* This is a percent increase problem. So we will use the formula for percent change. The **original** value is 28. The new value is 35, so that the

change is 7. Using the percent change formula, we get that the percent increase is 7/28 * 100 = 25%, choice (C).

Warning: Don't accidently use the new value for "change" in the formula. The **change** is the positive difference between the original and new values.

LEVEL 3: PERCENTS

53. During a sale at a retail store, if a customer buys one t-shirt at full price, the customer is given a 25 percent discount on a second t-shirt of equal or lesser value. If John buys two t-shirts that have full prices of $30 and $20, by what percent is the total cost of the two t-shirts reduced during the sale? (Disregard the percent symbol when you grid your answer.)

* This is a percent decrease problem. So we will use the formula for percent change. The **original** cost of the two t-shirts is 30 + 20 = 50. The new cost is 30 + 15 = 45. Thus the **change** is 50 - 45 = 5. So the percent change is 5/50 * 100 = 10%. So we grid the answer **10**.

Note: To get the 15 in the second computation we need to discount 20 by 25 percent. Here are two ways to do that.

(1) Compute 25% of 20 = .25*20 = 5. Then subtract 20 − 5 = 15.
(2) Compute 75% of 20 = .75*20 = 15 (taking a 25% discount of something is the same as taking 75% of that thing).

Warning: Don't accidently use the new value for "change" in the formula. The **change** is the positive difference between the original and new values.

106

STRATEGY 13
REMAINDERS IN DISGUISE

$\mathcal{T}$o solve a problem that asks to find or use a remainder always begin with a number that is evenly divisible. Here is a simple example where the remainder is mentioned explicitly.

LEVEL 4: NUMBER THEORY

54. What is the least positive integer greater than 4 that leaves a remainder of 4 when divided by both 6 and 8?

* We first find the least positive integer greater than 4 that is divisible by both 6 and 8. This is the **least common multiple** of 6 and 8 which is 24. We now simply add the remainder.

$$24 + 4 = 28.$$

Thus, the answer is **28**.

Finding the least common multiple: Here are two ways to find the least common multiple of the given numbers.

(1) Start listing the multiples of the larger number until you get to a multiple of the smaller number.

8, 16, 24

We stop at 24 because it is also a multiple of 6.

(2) Here is a more sophisticated method that is much quicker if the least common multiple is large.

Step 1: Find the prime factorization of each number in the set.

$$6 = 2*3$$
$$8 = 2^3$$

Step 2: Choose the highest power of each prime that appears in any of the factorizations.

$$2^3 \text{ and } 3$$

Step 3: Multiply these numbers together to get the least common multiple.

$$2^3*3 = 24$$

LEVEL 3: NUMBER THEORY

55. Cards numbered from 1 through 2010 are distributed, one at a time, into nine stacks. The card numbered 1 is placed on stack 1, card number 2 on stack 2, card number 3 on stack 3, and so on until each stack has one card. If this pattern is repeated, each time beginning with stack one, on which stack will the card numbered 2010 be placed?

   (A) 1st stack
   (B) 2nd stack
   (C) 3rd stack
   (D) 4th stack
   (E) 5th stack

We first find an integer as close as possible to 2010 that is divisible by 9. We can check this in our calculator.

108

2010/9 ~ 223.33
2009/9 ~ 223.22
2008/9 ~ 223.11
2007/9 = 223

The last computation gave an integer. Therefore 2007 is divisible by 9. So card number 2007 will go on the 9th stack. Card 2008 will go on the 1st stack, card 2009 will go on the 2nd stack, and card 2010 will go on the 3rd stack. Thus, the answer is choice (C).

Remark: Notice that the word remainder is never mentioned in this problem. It is a remainder problem in disguise.

The divisibility by 9 trick: An integer is divisible by 9 precisely when the sum of its digits is divisible by 9.

2010 **is not** divisible by 9 because 2 + 0 + 1 + 0 = 3
2009 **is not** divisible by 9 because 2 + 0 + 0 + 9 = 11
2008 **is not** divisible by 9 because 2 + 0 + 0 + 8 = 10
2007 **is** divisible by 9 because 2 + 0 + 0 + 7 = 9

Other divisibility tricks: Here are some more divisibility tricks. Note that they have nothing to do with the given problem.

An integer is divisible by 2 precisely when the last digit is 0, 2, 4, 6 or 8.
An integer is divisible by 3 precisely when the sum of its digits are divisible by 3.
An integer is divisible by 4 precisely when the number formed by taking just the last two digits of the integer is divisible by 4.
An integer is divisible by 5 precisely when the last digit is 0 or 5.
An integer is divisible by 6 if it is divisible by 2 and by 3.
An integer is divisible by 10 if it ends in a 0.

* Quick computation using your calculator: Divide 2010 by 9 to get 2010/9 ~ 223.33. Now take the integer part of the answer and multiply by 9. We get 223*9 = 2007. Subtract this result from 2010 to get the remainder: 2010 – 2007 = 3. So the answer is choice (C).

Note: See page 51 for the calculator algorithm that was used in the last solution.

LEVEL 4: NUMBER THEORY

56. In the repeating decimal

$$0.\overline{123456} = 0.123456123456123456...$$

where the digits 123456 repeat, which digit is in the 5000th place to the right of the decimal?

(A) 1
(B) 2
(C) 3
(D) 4
(E) 5

Since there are exactly 6 digits before repeating we look for the remainder when 5000 is divided by 6. To do this, we first find an integer as close to 5000 as possible that is divisible by 6. We check this in our calculator.

5000/6 ~ 833.333
4999/6 ~ 833.167
4998/6 = 833

So 4998 is divisible by 6 and therefore 5000 gives a remainder of 2 when divided by 6. So the digit in the 5000th place is the same as the digit in the second place to the right of the decimal point. This is 2. Thus, the answer is choice (B).

* **Quick computation using your calculator:** Divide 5000 by 6 to get 5000/6 ~ 833.333. Now take the integer part of the answer and multiply by 6. We get 833*6 = 4998. Subtract this result from 5000 to get the remainder: 5000 − 4998 = 2. So the answer is choice (B).

Note: See page 51 for the calculator algorithm that was used in the last solution.

STRATEGY 14
SETTING UP
A RATIO

Step 1: Identify two key words and write them down one over the other.

Step 2: Next to each of these key words write down the numbers, variables or expressions that correspond to each key word in two columns.

Step 3: Draw in 2 division symbols and an equal sign.

Step 4: Cross multiply and divide.

This procedure is best understood by looking at some examples.

LEVEL 1: NUMBER THEORY

57. The sales tax on an $8.00 shirt is $0.60. At this rate what would be the sales tax on a $12.00 shirt?

    (A) $0.40
    (B) $0.60
    (C) $0.80
    (D) $0.90
    (E) $0.95

We begin by identifying 2 key words. In this case, such a pair of key words is "shirt" and "tax."

| shirt | 8 | 12 |
| tax | 0.60 | x |

Choose the words that are most helpful to you. Notice that we wrote in the shirt prices next to the word shirt, and the tax prices next to the word tax. Also notice that the tax for an $8 shirt is written under the number 8, and the (unknown) tax for a $12 shirt is written under the 12. Now draw in the division symbols and equal sign, cross multiply and divide the corresponding ratio to find the unknown quantity x.

$$8/.060 = 12/x$$
$$8x = 12*0.60$$
$$8x = 7.2$$
$$x = 0.90$$

So the tax on a $12 shirt is $0.90. Thus the answer is choice (D).

* **Mental math:** If the tax on an $8.00 shirt is $0.60, then the tax on a $4.00 shirt would be $0.30 at this rate. Thus, the tax on a $12.00 shirt would be $0.90, choice (D).

LEVEL 1: ALGEBRA

58. Running at a constant speed, a cheetah traveled 200 miles in 5 hours. At this rate, how many miles did the cheetah travel in 4 hours?

As in the last problem we identify 2 key words. This time let's choose "miles" and "hours."

| miles | 200 | x |
| hours | 5 | 4 |

We now find x by cross multiplying and dividing.

$$200/5 = x/4$$
$$800 = 5x$$
$$x = 800/5 = \textbf{160}.$$

Alternate solution: Using d = r*t (distance = rate * time), we have

$$200 = r*5$$
$$r = 200/5 = 40 \text{ mph}$$

Using d = r*t again, we have d = 40*4 = **160**.

* **Mental math:** 200 miles in 5 hours is 40 miles per hour (divide 200 by 5). Thus, the cheetah travelled 4*40 = **160** miles in 4 hours.

LEVEL 2: NUMBER THEORY

59. A copy machine makes 4800 copies per hour. At this rate, in how many <u>minutes</u> can the copy machine produce 920 copies?

We identify 2 key words. Let's choose "copies" and "minutes."

copies	4800	920
minutes	60	x

At first glance it might seem to make more sense to choose "hours" as our second key word, but choosing the word "minutes" is more efficient because

(a) The answer that we're looking for must be in minutes.
(b) It's extremely simple to convert 1 hour into 60 minutes.

We now find x by cross multiplying and dividing.

$$4800/60 = 920/x$$
$$4800x = 55200$$
$$x = 11.5$$

So, the answer is **11.5**.

* **Quick computation:** (920/4800)*60 = **11.5**.

LEVEL 3: GEOMETRY

60. The height of a solid cone is 22 centimeters and the radius of the base is 15 centimeters. A cut parallel to the circular base is made completely through the cone so that one of the two resulting solids is a smaller cone. If the radius of the base of the small cone is 5 centimeters, what is the height of the small cone, in centimeters?

* **Quick computation:** For those students that are getting the hang of this, here's the quick computation right away: **(22/15)*5 = 22/3** or **7.33**.

Detailed solution. A picture of the problem looks like this:

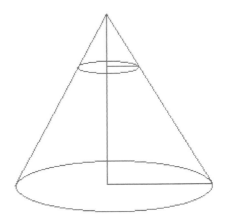

In the above picture we have the original cone together with a cut forming a smaller cone. We have also drawn two triangles that represent the 2 dimensional cross sections of the 2 cones. Let's isolate the triangles:

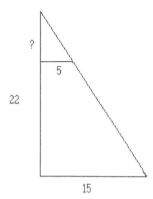

The two triangles formed are **similar**, and so the ratios of their sides are equal. We identify the 2 key words "height" and "radius."

height	22	h	
radius	15	5	

We now find h by cross multiplying and dividing.

$$22/15 = h/5$$
$$110 = 15h$$
$$h \sim 7.333333$$

So we grid in **7.33**.

Notes: (1) The answer would be marked wrong if we were to grid in 7.3. We need to use all four slots in the grid when rounding or truncating a decimal.

(2) We can also grid in the fraction **22/3**.

Definition: Two triangles are **similar** if they have the same angles.

Notes: (1) To show that two triangles are similar we need only show that two angles of one of the triangles are equal to two angles of the other triangle (the third is free because all triangles have 180 degrees).

(2) Similar triangles do not have to be the same size.

(3) Similar triangles have sides that are all in the same proportion.

115

STRATEGY 15
CHANGE FRACTIONS TO DECIMALS

*D*ecimals are often easier to work with than fractions, especially since you have a calculator. To change a fraction to a decimal you simply perform the division in your calculator.

LEVEL 1: NUMBER THEORY

61. Which of the following groups contains three fractions that are equal?

(A) $\dfrac{1}{3}, \dfrac{1}{6}, \dfrac{1}{9}$

(B) $\dfrac{2}{3}, \dfrac{4}{6}, \dfrac{6}{8}$

(C) $\dfrac{2}{5}, \dfrac{4}{25}, \dfrac{8}{125}$

(D) $\dfrac{2}{5}, \dfrac{6}{15}, \dfrac{10}{25}$

(E) $\dfrac{2}{5}, \dfrac{6}{15}, \dfrac{10}{20}$

* We begin with choice (C), and change each fraction to a decimal by dividing in our calculator.

$$2/5 = .4 \quad 4/25 = .16$$

Since these decimals disagree there is no reason to continue, and we eliminate choice (C). Let's try choice (D) next.

$$2/5 = .4 \qquad 6/15 = .4 \qquad 10/25 = .4$$

Since these are all the same, the answer is choice (D).

Note: There is no actual advantage to starting with choice (C) in this problem, but there is no disadvantage either. We should always start with choice (C) just so we are in the habit of doing so (unless one of the words greatest or least appears in the problem as mentioned in strategy 2 above).

LEVEL 2: ALGEBRA

62. What number increased by 5 equals 4 times the number?

   (A) 0

   (B) $\dfrac{3}{5}$

   (C) $\dfrac{4}{5}$

   (D) $\dfrac{5}{3}$

   (E) 9

We will combine the method of changing fractions to decimals with the method of starting with choice (C).

Let's change the numbers to decimals by dividing in our calculators. The answer choices then become the following.

   (A) 0
   (B) 0.6
   (C) 0.8
   (D) Approximately 1.67
   (E) 9

Begin by looking at choice (C). Increase 0.8 by 5 to get 0.8 + 5 = 5.8. 4 times 0.8 is 4*0.8 = 3.2. Since we got two different numbers, (C) is not the answer.

Let's try (D) next. When we increase 1.67 by 5 we get 1.67 + 5 = 6.67. 4 times 1.67 is 6.68.

Since we **approximated** 5/3 as 1.67, the answer is (D).

To be positive that this is the correct answer we can either check that the other 3 answers do **not work**, or we can do the same computation in the calculator with 5/3 instead of 1.67.

* **An algebraic solution for the advanced student:** Let's name the number. We'll call it x.

The number increased by 5 is x + 5.
4 times the number is 4x.

Thus we have x + 5 = 4x. We subtract x from both sides of the equation to get 5 = 3x. Dividing by 3 gives us 5/3 = x. This is choice (D).

LEVEL 4: NUMBER THEORY

63.   What is one possible value of x for which $\dfrac{1}{4} < x < \dfrac{3}{11}$?

* It is quite difficult to find a fraction between these two directly, but the problem becomes much easier if we convert these two fractions to decimals. To do this we simply divide 1 by 4, and 3 by 11 in our calculators.

1/4 = .25   3/11 ~ .2727 (where ~ means "is approximately")

So **.26** is a possible answer.

Note: There are several other answers such as

.251, .252, ... , .259, .261, .262, ..., .269, .27, .271 and .272.

STRATEGY 16
TRY A SIMPLE OPERATION

*P*roblems that ask for an expression involving more than one variable often look much harder than they are. By performing a single operation, the problem is usually reduced to one that is very easy to solve. The most common operations to try are addition, subtraction, multiplication and division.

LEVEL 3: ALGEBRA

$$
\begin{array}{r}
3 \\
2a \\
5 \\
b \\
7 \\
+9 \\
\hline
75
\end{array}
\qquad
\begin{array}{r}
3 \\
a \\
5 \\
c \\
7 \\
+9 \\
\hline
61
\end{array}
$$

64. In the correctly worked addition problems above, what is the value of $a + b - c$?

Let's rewrite the equations horizontally since that is how most of us are used to seeing equations.

$$3 + 2a + 5 + b + 7 + 9 = 75$$
$$3 + a + 5 + c + 7 + 9 = 61$$

The operation to use here is subtraction. Let's go ahead and subtract term by term.

$$3 + 2a + 5 + b + 7 + 9 = 75$$
$$\underline{3 + a + 5 + c + 7 + 9 = 61}$$
$$a + (b - c) = 14$$

So a + b − c = **14**.

Remark: Whenever we are trying to find an expression that involves addition, subtraction, or both, **adding or subtracting** the given equations usually does the trick.

* Visualizing the answer: You can save a substantial amount of time by performing the subtraction in your head (left equation minus right equation). Note that above the lines the subtraction yields a + b − c. This is exactly what we're looking for. Thus, we need only subtract below the lines to get the answer: 75 − 61 = **14**.

An **alternate solution by picking numbers:** If we choose any value for a, then b and c will be determined. So, let's set a equal to 0. Then

$$3 + 5 + b + 7 + 9 = 75$$
$$24 + b = 75$$
$$b = 51$$

$$3 + 5 + c + 7 + 9 = 61$$
$$24 + c = 61$$
$$c = 37$$

So a + b − c = 0 + 51 − 37 = 14. Thus, the answer is **14**.

Remark: Any choice for a will give us the same answer. We could have chosen a value for b or c as well. But once we choose a value for one of the variables the other two are determined.

LEVEL 3: ALGEBRA

65. If $ab = 3$, $bc = 4$, $b^2 = \dfrac{1}{7}$, what is the value of ac?

* The operation to use here is multiplication.

$$ab = 3$$
$$\underline{bc = 4}$$
$$(ab)(bc) = 3*4$$
$$ab^2c = 12$$

Now substitute 1/7 in for b^2. So we have a(1/7)c = 12. Multiplying both sides of the equation by 7 gives us ac = 12*7 = **84**.

Remark: Whenever we are trying to find an expression that involves multiplication, division, or both, **multiplying or dividing** the given equations usually does the trick.

Note: If we had multiplied all 3 equations together we would have gotten $ab^4c = 12/7$. This isn't as efficient, but it still works. Note that

$b^4 = b^2b^2 = (1/7)*(1/7) = 1/49$. Thus, ac = (12/7) * 49 = **84**.

LEVEL 5: ALGEBRA

66. If $xy = 5$, $yz = 8$, $xz = 10$, and $x > 0$, then $xyz =$

The operation to use here is multiplication.

$$xy = 5$$
$$yz = 8$$
$$\underline{xz = 10}$$
$$(xy)(yz)(xz) = 5*8*10$$
$$x^2y^2z^2 = 400$$

Notice that we multiply all three left hand sides together, and all three right hand sides together. Now just take the square root of both sides of the equation to get xyz = 20. Thus, the answer is **20**.

Remark: Whenever we are trying to find an expression that involves multiplication, division, or both, **multiplying or dividing** the given equations usually does the trick.

* Quick computation: With a little practice, we can get the solution to this type of problem very quickly. Here, we multiply the three numbers together to get 5*8*10 = 400 We then take the square root of 400 to get **20**.

LEVEL 5: ALGEBRA

67. If $x^8 = \dfrac{3}{z}$, and $x^7 = \dfrac{3y}{z}$, which of the following is an expression for x in terms of y ?

(A) $3y$

(B) $2y$

(C) y

(D) $\dfrac{1}{y}$

(E) $\dfrac{3}{y}$

* The operation to use here is division. We divide the left hand sides of each equation, and the right hand sides of each equation. First the left. Recall that when we divide expressions with the same base we need to subtract the exponents. Therefore $x^8/x^7 = x^1 = x$. Now for the right. Recall that dividing is the same as multiplying by the reciprocal. So, (3/z)/(3y/z) = (3/z)*(z/3y) = 1/y. Thus, x = 1/y and the answer is choice (D).

Alternate Solution: Multiply both sides of each equation by z to get

$$zx^8 = 3$$
$$zx^7 = 3y$$

Multiplying both sides of the second equation by x yields

$$zx^8 = 3xy$$

So
$$3xy = 3$$
$$xy = 1$$
$$x = 1/y$$

Thus, the answer is choice (D).

LEVEL 5: ALGEBRA

68. If $3x = 1 + 2y$ and $4x = 2 - 3y$, what is the value of x?

* Since we are trying to find x, we want to make y go away. So we make the two coefficients of y "match up" by multiplying by the appropriate numbers. We will multiply the first equation by 3 and the second equation by 2.

$$3*(3x) = (1 + 2y)*3$$
$$2*(4x) = (2 - 3y)*2$$

$$9x = 3 + 6y$$
$$8x = 4 - 6y$$

We now add the two equations.

$$9x = 3 + 6y$$
$$\underline{8x = 4 - 6y}$$
$$17x = 7$$

Now divide both sides by 17 to get x = **7/17**.

Remark: If we divide 7 by 17 in our calculator, we get 7/17 ~ .4117647. Thus we can also grid in **.411** or **.412** (the first decimal is truncated, the second is rounded). Note that gridding in .41 will result in getting the answer incorrect.

LEVEL 2: ALGEBRA

69. If $5x + y = 12$ and $3x + y = 14$, what is the value of $4x + y$?

* We add the two equations to get

$$5x + y = 12$$
$$\underline{3x + y = 14}$$
$$8x + 2y = 26$$

Now observe that 8x + 2y = 2(4x + y). So 4x + y = 26/2 = **13**.

Remark: Notice that although this is only a Level 2 question, it appears to be of the same difficulty of a Level 5 question when this method is used. It is easier in this problem to solve the system of equations. That is it is easier to find x and y individually and then substitute those values in for 4x + y. This is however more time consuming than the method we just used.

LEVEL 3: ALGEBRA

70. If $10x + 20y = 57$, what is the value of $x + 2y$?

* We divide both sides of the equation by 10 to get x + 2y = **5.7**.

Note: When we divide the left hand side by 10, we have to divide **each** term by 10.

$$10x/10 = x \qquad\qquad 20y/10 = 2y$$

Alternative: We can factor out 10 on the left hand side

$$10x + 20y = 10(x + 2y).$$

So we have

$$10x + 20y = 57$$
$$10(x + 2y) = 57$$
$$x + 2y = \textbf{5.7}$$

STRATEGY 17
FIND THE PATTERN
IN A SEQUENCE

$\mathcal{T}$o find the pattern in a sequence we simply begin writing out the sequence, and keep writing until we see the pattern clearly.

LEVEL 5: NUMBER THEORY

71. The first two numbers of a sequence are 2 and 5, respectively. The third number is 7, and, in general, every number after the second is the sum of the two numbers immediately preceding it. How many of the first 500 numbers in the sequence are odd?

    (A) 166
    (B) 167
    (C) 332
    (D) 333
    (E) 334

* Start writing out the terms of the sequence.

$$2, 5, 7, 12, 19, 31, 50, 81, 131, 212, ...$$

Notice that the pattern is even, odd, odd, even, odd, odd, ...

The greatest number less than 500 that is divisible by 3 is 498. So of the first 498 numbers in the sequence 2/3 * 498 = 332 are odd. The 499th

and 450th terms are even and odd, respectively, and therefore the answer is 332 + 1 = 333, choice (D).

Remark: Notice that this is also a "remainders in disguise" problem. We checked divisibility by 3 because the pattern repeats every third term. Any term which is divisible by 3 behaves like the third term of the sequence. Any term which has a remainder of 1 when divided by 3 behaves like the first term of the sequence. And any term which has a remainder of 2 when divided by 3 behaves like the second term of the sequence. Here is the sequence listed while keeping track of which remainder it goes with

remainder 1 (even)	remainder 2 (odd)	No remainder (odd)
2	5	7
12	19	31
50	81	131
212 ...	...	...
...		

STRATEGY 18
CHANGE FRACTIONAL PARTS TO WHOLES

*W*e can often change fractional parts to wholes by making the total equal to some multiple of the least common denominator of the fractions involved. If the problem is multiple choice use the denominators in the answer choices as a guide.

LEVEL 5: NUMBER THEORY

72. A business is owned by 1 man and 5 women, each of whom has an equal share. If one of the women sells $\frac{2}{5}$ of her share to the man, and another of the women keeps $\frac{1}{4}$ of her share and sells the rest to the man, what fraction of the business will the man own?

    (A) $\frac{9}{40}$

    (B) $\frac{37}{120}$

    (C) $\frac{2}{3}$

    (D) $\frac{43}{120}$

    (E) $\frac{3}{8}$

Using the answer choices as a guide we will split the business into 120 parts, so that each person has 120/6 = 20 parts. We have 2/5 * 20 = 8 and 3/4 * 20 = 15.   So after both sales the man has 20 + 8 + 15 = 43 parts out of 120 parts total. Thus, the answer is choice (D).

Remark: The number 120 comes from multiplying the least common denominator of the two fractions (5*4 = 20) by the number of people (6). That is, 20*6 = 120.

* Single computation: This is quick, but a bit tricky. Each of the 6 people begins with 1/6 of the business. The first woman sells 2/5 * 1/6 of the business, and the second woman sells 3/4 * 1/6 of the business (If she keeps 1/4, then she sells 3/4). Therefore we can get the answer by doing the following single computation in our calculator:

1/6 + 2/5 * 1/6 + 3/4 * 1/6 = 43/120, choice (D).

LEVEL 5: PROBABILITY & STATISTICS

73. A set of marbles contains only black marbles, white marbles, and yellow marbles. If the probability of randomly choosing a black marble is $\frac{1}{14}$ and the probability of randomly choosing a white marble is $\frac{3}{4}$, what is the probability of randomly choosing a yellow marble?

The least common denominator of the two fractions is 28, so we will assume that there are 28 marbles total. There are 1/14 * 28 = 2 black marbles, and 3/4 * 28 = 21 white marbles. So there are 28 − 2 − 21 = 5 yellow marbles, and the probability of choosing a yellow marble is 5/28. So we can grid in **5/28**.

We can also divide in our calculator to get 5/28 ~ .17857. We can truncate this to **.178**, or round it to **.179** and grid in either of these two decimals.

Note: Instead of using the least common denominator we could have simply multiplied the denominators together to get 14*4 = 56. There would then be 1/14 * 56 = 4 black marbles, 3/4 *56 = 42 white marbles, and therefore 56 – 4 – 42 = 10 yellow marbles. Thus the probability of choosing a yellow marble is 10/56. Since there are too many symbols to grid in, we must reduce this fraction or change it to a decimal.

Remark for the more advanced student: The **least common denominator** is simply the **least common multiple** of the denominators. Here is a quick way to find the least common multiple of a set of positive integers (we will use the 2 denominators in the problem as an example).

Step 1: Find the prime factorization of each integer in the set.

$$14 = 2*7$$
$$4 = 2^2$$

Step 2: Choose the highest power of each prime that appears in any of the factorizations.

$$2^2 \text{ and } 7$$

Step 3: Multiply these numbers together to get the least common multiple.

$$2^2*7 = 28$$

* A quick solution: Since probabilities add up to one, the probability of randomly choosing a yellow marble is $1 - 1/14 - 3/4 \sim .1785714286$ (this computation was done in a calculator). Thus, we can grid in **.178**, **.179**, or the fraction **5/28**.

STRATEGY 19
RECOGNIZE BLOCKS

*L*et's define a **block** to be an algebraic expression that appears more than once in a given problem. Very often in SAT problems a block can be treated just like a variable. In particular, blocks should usually not be manipulated—treat them as a single unit.

LEVEL 1: ALGEBRA

74.   If $7(a+b)-5=37$, then $a+b=$

There is a block of **a + b**. Let's look at a seemingly easier problem:

If 7x – 5 = 37, then x =

We can guess values for x until we get the right answer.

x	7x – 5	
3	7*3 – 5 = 21 – 5 = 16	too small
5	7*5 – 5 = 35 – 5 = 30	still too small
7	7*7 – 5 = 49 – 5 = 44	too big
6	7*6 – 5 = 42 – 5 = 37	correct

Thus, the answer is **6**.

But this is essentially the same problem as the one we were given. We just replaced the block by the variable x. So the answer to the original question is also **6**.

Alternative: Instead of guessing values for x, we can simply perform the algebra.

$$7x - 5 = 37$$
$$7x = 42$$
$$x = \mathbf{6}.$$

* Mental math: We can do the whole computation in our head very quickly. Simply add 5 to 37, and then divide by 7 to get the answer.

$$a + b = (37 + 5)/7 = 42/7 = \mathbf{6}.$$

LEVEL 2: ALGEBRA

75. If $3x - 5y = 7$, what is the value of $6(3x - 5y)$?

   (A) 50
   (B) 42
   (C) 36
   (D) 30
   (E) 4

In this example there is a block of **3x − 5y**. Let's look at the following seemingly easier problem:

If a = 7, what is the value of 6a?

The answer to this problem is 6*7 = 42.

But this is essentially the same problem as the one we were given. We just replaced the block by the variable a. So the answer to the original question is also 42, choice (B).

* Mental math: This problem can be done in just a few seconds.

$$6*7 = 42, \text{ choice (B)}.$$

LEVEL 4: PROBABILITY & STATISTICS

76. If $b = 7(\dfrac{u+v+x+y+z}{5})$, then in terms of b, what is the average (arithmetic mean) of u, v, x, y, and z ?

    (A) $\dfrac{b}{35}$

    (B) $\dfrac{b}{7}$

    (C) $\dfrac{b}{5}$

    (D) $5b$

    (E) $7b$

* In this example there is a block of **a = (u + v + x + y + z)/5** which is precisely the average of u, v, x, y, and z. So solving this problem is the same as solving the following equation for a.

$$b = 7a$$

To solve this equation for a we simply divide both of the sides by 7 to get a = b/7, choice (B).

STRATEGY 20
CHANGE AVERAGES
TO SUMS

A problem involving averages often becomes much easier when we first convert the averages to sums. We can easily change an average to a sum using the following simple formula.

Sum = Average * Number

Many problems with averages involve one or more conversions to sums, followed by a subtraction.

Note: The above formula comes from eliminating the denominator in the definition of average.

$$\text{Average} = \frac{\text{Sum}}{\text{Number}}$$

133

LEVEL 1: PROBABILITY & STATISTICS

77. The average (arithmetic mean) of three numbers is 100. If two of the numbers are 80 and 130, what is the third number?

   (A) 70
   (B) 80
   (C) 90
   (D) 100
   (E) 110

* In this case we are averaging 3 numbers. Thus the Number is 3. The Average is given to be 100. So the Sum of the 3 numbers is 100*3 = 300. Since we know that two of the numbers are 80 and 130, the third number is 300 − 80 − 130 = 90, choice (C).

LEVEL 3: PROBABILITY & STATISTICS

78. The average (arithmetic mean) of seven numbers is 10. When an eighth number is added, the average of the eight numbers is also 10. What is the eighth number?

   (A) 0
   (B) $\dfrac{4}{5}$
   (C) $\dfrac{5}{4}$
   (D) 8
   (E) 10

* The sum of the seven numbers is 10*7 = 70.
The sum of the eight numbers is 10*8 = 80.
The eighth number is 80 − 70 = 10, choice (E).

LEVEL 4: PROBABILITY & STATISTICS

79. If the average (arithmetic mean) of k and $k+3$ is b and if the average of k and $k-3$ is c, what is the average of b and c?

    (A) 1

    (B) $\dfrac{k}{2}$

    (C) k

    (D) $k+\dfrac{1}{2}$

    (E) $2k$

* The sum of k and k + 3 is k + (k + 3) = 2k + 3, so that 2k + 3 = 2b. The sum of k and k − 3 is k + (k − 3) = 2k − 3 so that 2k − 3 = 2c. So,

$$2b + 2c = 4k$$
$$2(b + c) = 4k$$
$$(b + c)/2 = k.$$

Thus, the answer is choice (C).

Alternative solution by picking numbers: Let's choose a value for k, say k = 5. Then k + 3 = 8 and k − 3 = 2. So,

$$b = (5 + 8)/2 = 13/2 = 6.5$$
$$c = (5 + 2) /2 = 7/2 = 3.5$$

and the average of b and c is (b + c)/2 = (6.5 + 3.5)/2 = 10/2 = **5. Put a nice big, dark circle around this number so that you can find it easily later.** We now substitute k = 5 into each answer choice.

(A) 1
(B) 2.5
(C) 5
(D) 5.5
(E) 10

We now compare each of these numbers to the number that we put a nice big, dark circle around. Since (A), (B), (D) and (E) are incorrect we can eliminate them. Therefore the answer is choice (C).

Important note: (C) is **not** the correct answer simply because it is equal to 5. It is correct because all 4 of the other choices are **not** 5. **You absolutely must check all five choices!**

LEVEL 5: PROBABILITY & STATISTICS

80. The average (arithmetic mean) salary of employees at a bank with A employees in thousands of dollars is 53, and the average salary of employees at a bank with B employees in thousands of dollars is 95. When the salaries of both banks are combined, the average salary in thousands of dollars is 83. What is the value of $\dfrac{A}{B}$?

* The sum of the salaries of employees at bank A (in thousands) is 53A. The sum of the salaries of employees at bank B (in thousands) is 95B.

Adding these we get the sum of the salaries of all employees (in thousands): 53A + 95B.

We can also get this sum directly from the problem.

$$83(A + B) = 83A + 83B.$$

So we have that 53A + 95B = 83A + 83B.

We get A to one side of the equation by subtracting 53A from both sides, and we get B to the other side by subtracting 83B from both sides.

$$12B = 30A$$

We can get A/B to one side by performing **cross division.** We do this just like cross multiplication, but we divide instead. Dividing both sides of the equation by 30B will do the trick (this way we get rid of B on the left, and 30 on the right).

$$A/B = 12/30 = \mathbf{2/5}$$

So we can grid in **2/5** or **.4**.

LEVEL 5: PROBABILITY & STATISTICS

81. A group of students take a test and the average score is 65. One more student takes the test and receives a score of 92 increasing the average score of the group to 68. How many students were in the initial group?

* Let n be the number of students in the initial group. We change the average to a sum using the formula Sum = Average * Number

So the initial sum is 65n.

When we take into account the new student, we can find the new sum in two different ways.

(1) We can add the new score to the old sum to get 65n + 92.
(2) We can compute the new sum directly using the simple formula above to get 68(n + 1) = 68n + 68.

We now set these equal to each other and solve for n:

$$65n + 92 = 68n + 68$$
$$24 = 3n$$
$$n = \mathbf{8}.$$

STRATEGY 21
WHEN WRITING A LIST USE A CLEAR AND DEFINITE PATTERN

Sometimes the easiest way to count the number of possibilities is to simply list them all. When doing this it is important to have a systematic way of forming our list. This will reduce the likelihood of missing something, or listing something twice.

LEVEL 3: COUNTING

82. How many integers between 9 and 500 have the tens digit equal to 2, 3, or 4 and the units digit (ones digit) equal to 5 or 6?

Let's try to list the numbers in **increasing order**.

25	26	35	36	45	46
125	126	135	136	145	146
225	226	235	236	245	246
325	326	335	336	345	346
425	426	435	436	445	446

And that's it. We see that the answer is 6*5 = **30**.

Remark: We can get the answer quicker by using the **counting principle** instead of actually listing every possibility. There are 2 possibilities for the ones digit (5 or 6). There are 3 possibilities for the tens digit (2, 3, or 4). There are 5 possibilities for the hundreds digit (0, 1, 2, 3 or 4).

* The counting principle says that we multiply the possibilities to get 2*3*5 = **30**.

LEVEL 3: COUNTING

83. Three light bulbs are placed into three different lamps. How many different arrangements are possible for three light bulbs of different colors – one white, one red, and one green?

We list all the possibilities:

white	red	green
white	green	red
red	white	green
red	green	white
green	white	red
green	red	white

We can easily see that there are **6** arrangements.

Remarks: When you actually write out this list you should use abbreviations such as "w" for white, "r" for red, and "g" for green. This will save some time.

* A more sophisticated solution without listing: We can count the arrangements without actually making a list. There are 3 light bulbs, and we are arranging all 3 of them. So there are $_3P_3$ = 3! = 1*2*3 = **6** arrangements.

Permutations: $_3P_3$ means the number of **permutations** of 3 things taken 3 at a time. In a permutation order matters (as opposed to the **combination** $_3C_3$ where the order does not matter).

$$_3P_3 = 3!/0! = (1*2*3)/1 = 6$$

In general, if n is an integer, then n! = 1*2*3*...*n
If n and k are integers, then $_nP_r$ = n!/(n-r)!

On the SAT you do **not** need to know these formulas. You can do these computations very quickly on your graphing calculator. For example, to compute $_3P_3$, type 3 into your calculator, then in the **Math** menu scroll over to **Prb** and select **nPr** (or press **2**). Then type 3 and hit **Enter**. You will get an answer of 6.

LEVEL 4: GEOMETRY

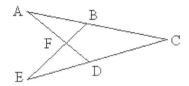

84. Segments AC, AD, BE, and EC intersect at the labeled points as shown in the figure above. Define two points as "dependent" if they lie on the same segment in the figure. Of the labeled points in the figure, how many pairs of dependent points are there?

(A) None
(B) Three
(C) Six
(D) Nine
(E) Twelve

Let's list the dependent pairs of points.

A,F	F,D	A,D
E,F	F,B	E,B
A,B	B,C	A,C
E,D	D,C	E,C

So there are twelve pairs of dependent points, choice (E).

Note: Notice that our list follows a definite pattern. Here we took one long line segment at a time, and listed first the two pairs of points adjoining the two shorter segments, and then the pair adjoining the long segment.

* A more sophisticated solution without listing: We can count the pairs without actually making a list. There are 4 line segments, each with 3 points. So each segment has $_3C_2$ = 3 pairs of dependent points. So there are 4*3 = 12 pairs of dependent points all together, choice (E).

Combinations: $_3C_2$ means the number of **combinations** of 3 things taken 2 at a time. In a combination order does not matter (as opposed to the **permutation** $_3P_2$ where the order does matter).

$$_3P_2 = 3!/1! = (1*2*3)/1 = 6$$
$$_3C_2 = 3!/2!1! = (1*2*3)/(1*2) = 6/2 = 3$$

In general, if n is an integer, then n! = 1*2*3*...*n
If n and k are integers, then $_nP_r$ = n!/(n-r)! and $_nC_r$ = n!/[r!(n-r)!]

On the SAT you do **not** need to know these formulas. You can do these computations very quickly on your graphing calculator. For example, to compute $_3C_2$, type 3 into your calculator, then in the **Math** menu scroll over to **Prb** and select **nCr** (or press **3**). Then type 2 and hit **Enter**. You will get an answer of 3.

STRATEGY 22
MOVE THE SIDES OF A FIGURE AROUND

A seemingly difficult geometry problem can sometimes be made much easier by moving the sides of the figure around.

A classic example of this on the SAT is when you have two intersecting right triangles.

LEVEL 5: GEOMETRY

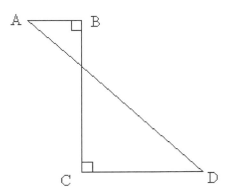

Note: Figure not drawn to scale.

85. In the figure above, $AB = 2, BC = 8$, and $AD = 10$. What is the length of line segment CD?

* The problem becomes much simpler if we "move" BC to the left and AB to the bottom as shown below.

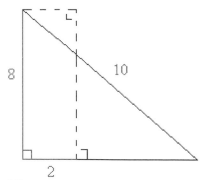

Note: Figure not drawn to scale.

We now have a single right triangle and we can either use the Pythagorean Theorem, or better yet notice that 10 = 5*2 and 8 = 4*2. Thus the other leg of the triangle is 3*2 = 6. So we see that CD must have length 6 – 2 = **4**.

Remark: If we didn't notice that this was a multiple of a 3-4-5 triangle, then we would use the Pythagorean Theorem as follows.

$$(x + 2)^2 + 8^2 = 10^2$$
$$(x + 2)^2 + 64 = 100$$
$$(x + 2)^2 = 36$$
$$x + 2 = 6$$
$$x = \mathbf{4}$$

Here is an easier geometry problem where the same technique works.

143

LEVEL 2: GEOMETRY

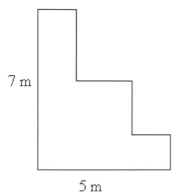

7 m

5 m

Note: Figure not drawn to scale.

86.   What is the perimeter, in meters, of the figure above?

* Recall that to compute the perimeter of the figure we need to add up the lengths of all 8 line segments in the figure. We "move" the two smaller horizontal segments up and the two smaller vertical segments to the right as shown below.

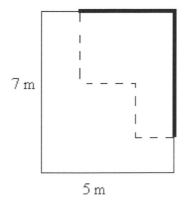

7 m

5 m

Note: Figure not drawn to scale.

Note that the "bold" length is equal to the "dashed" length. Thus, the perimeter is

$$2*7 + 2*5 = 14 + 10 = \textbf{24}.$$

Warning: Although lengths remain unchanged by moving line segments around, areas will be changed. This method should **not** be used in problems involving areas.

STRATEGY 23
AREAS OF
SHADED REGIONS

$\mathcal{F}$inding the area of a shaded region often involves subtracting two areas. The area formulas that you need are either formulas that are given to you in the front of the section or are given in the problem itself.

LEVEL 5: GEOMETRY

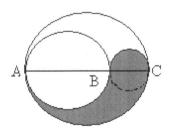

Note: Figure not drawn to scale

87. AB, BC, and AC are diameters of the three circles shown above. If $BC = 4$ and $AB = 5BC$, what is the area of the shaded region?

    (A) 48π
    (B) 24π
    (C) 12π
    (D) 6π
    (E) 3π

* We first find the radii of each of the three circles. The diameter of the small circle is 4, and so its radius is 2. The diameter of the medium-sized circle is 5*4 = 20, and so its radius is 10. The diameter of the largest circle is 20 + 4 = 24, and so its radius is 12. We can now find the area of the shaded region as follows.

Area = ½ (Area of big circle) – ½ (Area of medium circle) + ½ (Area of small circle)

= ½ (π*12²) – ½ (π*10²) + ½ (π*2²)

= ½ (π*144) – ½ (π*100) + ½ (π*4)

= ½ *48π

= 24π

Thus, the answer is choice (B).

LEVEL 4: GEOMETRY

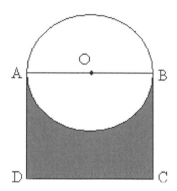

88.   In the figure above, AB is a diameter of the circle with center O and $ABCD$ is a square. What is the area of the shaded region if the radius of the circle is 7?

(A) $49(4 - \dfrac{\pi}{2})$

(B) $49(2 - \dfrac{\pi}{2})$

(C) $\pi(4 - \pi)$

(D) $\pi(2 - \pi)$

(E) $\pi(1 - \pi)$

* A side of the square has length x = 2r = 2*7 = 14. The area of the square is then x^2 = 14^2 =196.

The area of the circle is πr^2 = $\pi(7)^2$ = 49π. The area of the semicircle is then 49π/2. The area of the shaded region is

Area of Square – Area of Semicircle
196 – 49π/2
49(4 – π/2)

Thus, the answer is choice (A).

Note: As an alternative to factoring in the last step we can do the computation 196 – 49π/2 in the calculator to get **119.03098**. We then do the same with the answer choices until we get one that matches up. We would then see that choice (A) gives the same answer. Of course, this would be more time consuming, but it's better to be safe if you are not good at factoring, or you simply don't see that you need to factor.

STRATEGY 24

FITTING GEOMETRIC OBJECTS INSIDE ANOTHER OBJECT

*T*o see how many two-dimensional objects fit inside another two-dimensional object we divide areas. To see how many three-dimensional objects fit inside another three-dimensional object we divide volumes.

LEVEL 3: GEOMETRY

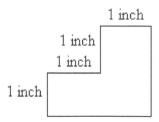

89. How many figures of the size and shape above are needed to completely cover a rectangle measuring 60 inches by 40 inches?

* The area of the given figure is 3 inches^2 and the area of the rectangle is 60*40 =2400 inches^2. We can see how many of the given figures cover the rectangle by dividing the two areas.

2400/3 = **800**.

Note: We can get the area of the given figure by splitting it into 3 squares each with area 1 inch^2 as shown below. Then 1 + 1 + 1 = 3

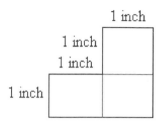

Another way to get the area of the given figure is to think of it as lying inside a square of side length 2 inches as shown below.

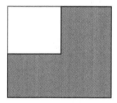

The area of the big square is 2*2 = 4 inches^2, and the area of the little square is 1*1 = 1 inch^2. So the area of the given figure is 4 − 1 = 3 inches^2. See Strategy 23 (areas of shaded regions) for more examples of this.

LEVEL 5: GEOMETRY

90. How many solid wood cubes, each with a total surface area of 150 square centimeters, can be cut from a solid wood cube with a total surface area of 1,350 square centimeters if no wood is lost in the cutting?

   (A) 3
   (B) 9
   (C) 27
   (D) 81
   (E) 243

* We get the surface area of a cube by adding up the areas of the 6 faces. Each face has area x^2 where x is the length of a side of the cube. Therefore the surface area of a cube is $6x^2$. So to get the length of a side of each cube we need to solve the equations

$$6x^2 = 150 \text{ and } 6x^2 = 1350$$
$$x^2 = 25 \qquad x^2 = 225$$
$$x = 5 \qquad x = 15$$

Thus the volume of each cube is $5^3 = 125$ and $15^3 = 3375$, respectively. We can see how many smaller cubes can be cut from the larger cube by dividing the two volumes.

$$3375/125 = 27, \text{ choice (C)}.$$

LEVEL 3: GEOMETRY

91. How many spherical snowballs with a radius of 3 centimeters can be made with the amount of snow in a spherical snowball of radius 6 centimeters? (the volume V of a sphere with radius r is given by $\frac{4}{3}\pi r^3$.)

* We divide the volumes: $(4/3 \, \pi*6^3)/(4/3 \, \pi*3^3) = 6^3/3^3 = 216/27 = $ **8**.

STRATEGY 25
KNOW THE
TRIANGLE RULE

*T*he **triangle rule** states that **the third side of a triangle is between the sum and difference of the other two sides**.

Make sure that you know this rule. Triangle rule problems are usually not that difficult but they tend to occur in hard problems because very few students know the rule.

LEVEL 5: GEOMETRY

92. If x is an integer greater than 5, how many different triangles are there with sides of length 3, 5 and x ?

  (A) One
  (B) Two
  (C) Three
  (D) Four
  (E) Five

* The triangle rule tells us that $5 - 3 < x < 5 + 3$. That is, $2 < x < 8$. Since x is an integer greater than 5, x can be 6 or 7. So there are **two** possibilities, choice (B).

LEVEL 5: GEOMETRY

93. Points A, B and C lie in a plane. If the distance between A and B is 7 and the distance between B and C is 4, which of the following could be the distance between A and C?

> I. 3
> II. 10
> III. 11

(A) I only
(B) II only
(C) III only
(D) I and III only
(E) I, II, and III

* In this case, if A, B and C form a triangle, then the length of AC is between 7 − 4 = 3 and 7 + 4 = 11. The extreme cases 3 and 11 form straight lines. In this problem that is fine, so the distance between A and C is between 3 and 11, inclusive. Thus, the answer is choice (E).

LEVEL 5: GEOMETRY

94. The lengths of the sides of a triangle are x, 8, and 15, where x is the shortest side. If the triangle is not isosceles, what is a possible value of x?

* The triangle rule tells us that 15 − 8 < x < 15 + 8. That is, 7 < x < 23. Since x is the shortest side, x < 8. So we must choose a number between 7 and 8. So we can grid in **7.1**.

Note: We can grid in any decimal or improper fraction between 7 and 8, but note that 7 and 8 are both **incorrect**.

STRATEGY 26
SIDES OPPOSITE BIGGER ANGLES ARE LONGER AND VICE VERSA

*I*n geometry problems sides of a geometric figure satisfy the same comparative relationships as their opposite angles.

LEVEL 4: GEOMETRY

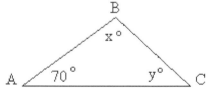

Note: Figure not drawn to scale.

95. In $\triangle ABC$ above, $AB > BC$. Which of the following must be true?

    (A) $AB = AC$
    (B) $AC < BC$
    (C) $x = y$
    (D) $x = 55$
    (E) $y > 55$

* Since AB > BC, the opposite angles to these sides share the same relationship. That is y > 70. So, 70 + y > 70 + 70 = 140, and x must be less

154

than 40. Since x is the smallest angle, AC is the shortest side. In particular, AC < BC, choice (B).

For another example of this strategy see the alternate solution for problem 36.

STRATEGY 27
USING SPECIAL TRIANGLES

 ere are the two special triangles given on the SAT.

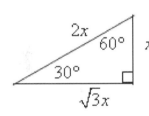 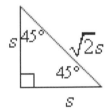

Some students get a bit confused because there are variables in these pictures. But the pictures become simplified if we substitute a 1 in for the variables. Then the sides of the 30, 60, 90 triangle are 1, 2 and $\sqrt{3}$ and the sides of the 45, 45, 90 triangle are 1, 1 and $\sqrt{2}$. The variable just tells us that if we multiply one of these sides by a number, then we have to multiply the other two sides by the same number. For example, instead of 1, 1 and $\sqrt{2}$, we can have 3, 3 and $3\sqrt{2}$ (here s = 3), or $\sqrt{2}$, $\sqrt{2}$, and 2 (here s = $\sqrt{2}$).

Also be aware that a 45, 45, 90 triangle is the same as an isosceles right triangle. Thus, if the two legs of a right triangle have the same length, we can use the 45, 45, 90 triangle to solve the problem, usually quite quickly.

LEVEL 4: GEOMETRY

96. What is the area of a square whose diagonal has length $4\sqrt{2}$?

We begin by drawing a picture

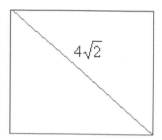

Since all sides of a square have equal length, an isosceles right triangle is formed. That is, it's a 45, 45, 90 triangle. So we can get the length of a side of the triangle just by looking at the formula. Here s is 4. The area of the square is then 4*4 = **16**.

Alternate solution using the Pythagorean Theorem: If we let x be the length of a side of the square, then by the Pythagorean Theorem

$$x^2 + x^2 = (4\sqrt{2})^2$$
$$2x^2 = 32$$
$$x^2 = 16$$
$$x = 4$$

Thus, the area of the square is 4*4 = **16**.

* Using an area formula: The area of a square is **$A = d^2/2$** where d is the length of the diagonal of the square. Therefore in this problem

$$A = d^2/2 = (4\sqrt{2})^2/2 = 32/2 = \mathbf{16}.$$

Exercise for the advanced student: Derive the area formula **$A = d^2/2$** using the more well-known area formula $A = (side)^2$ and the appropriate special triangle.

157

LEVEL 4: GEOMETRY

97. The length of each side of an equilateral triangle will be doubled to create a second triangle. The area of the second triangle will be how many times the area of the original triangle?

Let's let each side of the first triangle have length 2, so that each side of the second triangle has length 4. Recall that each angle of an equilateral triangle has 60 degrees. Thus, when we draw in the height of an equilateral triangles it is split into two 30, 60, 90 triangles as we see below.

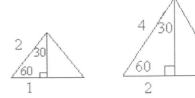

As we can see from the picture, the base of the smaller triangle is 1 and the base of the larger triangle is 2. Using the 30, 60, 90 triangle formula we see that the height of the smaller triangle is $\sqrt{3}$ and the height of the larger triangle is $2\sqrt{3}$. So, the area of the smaller triangle is

$$\tfrac{1}{2}*1*\sqrt{3} = \tfrac{1}{2}\sqrt{3}$$

and the area of the larger triangle is

$$\tfrac{1}{2}*2*2\sqrt{3} = 2\sqrt{3} .$$

We have to multiply the first area by 4 to get the second. So the answer is **4**.

Note: We don't actually need the exact value of the heights. If we call the height of the smaller triangle h, then the larger triangle has height 2h because the two right triangles are **similar** (they have the same angles). Therefore the area of the smaller triangle is ½*1*h = ½ h, and the area of the larger triangle is ½*2*2h = 2h. We need to multiply ½ h by 4 to get to 2h.

* A quick solution: Since we have to double the base and double the height of the smaller triangle to get to the larger triangle, the area is doubled twice, that is it is multiplied by **4**.

LEVEL 4: GEOMETRY

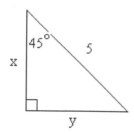

98.   In the triangle above, what is the value of $x + y$?

(A) 1

(B) $\dfrac{5\sqrt{2}}{2}$ (approximately 3.54)

(C) 5

(D) $5\sqrt{2}$ (approximately 7.07)

(E) 10

* Note that this is a 45, 45, 90 right triangle. Using the formula we see that x and y are both equal to s, and $s\sqrt{2} = 5$. Therefore

$$x + y = s + s = 5/\sqrt{2} + 5/\sqrt{2} \sim 7.07.$$

Thus, the answer is choice (D).

Remark: Without using a calculator we see that

$$x + y = 10/\sqrt{2} = (10\sqrt{2})/2 = 5\sqrt{2}.$$

As you can see it's much easier to just use the calculator.

Solution using the Pythagorean Theorem: Since two of the angles have equal measure (they both measure 45 degrees), the triangle is isosceles, and we see that x = y. By the Pythagorean Theorem

$$x^2 + x^2 = 5^2$$
$$2x^2 = 25$$
$$x^2 = 25/2$$
$$x = 5/\sqrt{2}$$

Therefore $x + y = x + x = 5/\sqrt{2} + 5/\sqrt{2} \sim 7.07$, choice (D).

LEVEL 5: GEOMETRY

99. A diagonal of a rectangle forms an angle of measure $30°$ with each of the two longer sides of the rectangle. If the length of the shorter side of the rectangle is 4, what is the length of the diagonal?

   (A) 10
   (B) 8
   (C) 6
   (D) $4\sqrt{3}$
   (E) $4\sqrt{2}$

* We begin by drawing a picture.

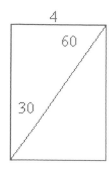

The side opposite 30 is 4. Thus the hypotenuse is 8, choice (B).

Note: The hypotenuse of a 30, 60, 90 triangle is always twice the length of the side opposite the 30 degree angle.

Also, if we always think of a side as going with its opposite angle, there will never be any confusion, even if our picture is facing a different direction than the triangle on the SAT. This is actually good advice for any triangle problem. Always think of a side in terms of its opposite angle and vice versa.

LEVEL 4: GEOMETRY

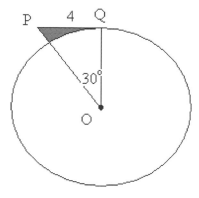

100. In the figure above, the center of the circle is O and $\overline{PQ}$ is tangent to the circle at Q. What is the area of the shaded region to the nearest tenth?

* A tangent line to a circle is perpendicular to the radius so that the triangle is a 30, 60, 90 right triangle. Since the side opposite 30 is 4, the side opposite 60 is $4\sqrt{3}$. In a right triangle we can think of the two legs as the base and the height. So the area of the triangle is

$$A = \tfrac{1}{2} \, bh = \tfrac{1}{2} \, 4 * 4\sqrt{3} = 8\sqrt{3}.$$

We already found that the radius of the circle is $4\sqrt{3}$. Thus the area of the circle is

$$A = \pi r^2 = \pi(4\sqrt{3})^2 = \pi * 16 * 3 = 48\pi.$$

The sector shown is 1/12 of the entire circle. So the area of the sector is

$$A = 1/12 * 48\pi = 4\pi.$$

The area of the shaded region is the area of the triangle minus the area of the sector.

$$A = 8\sqrt{3} - 4\pi \sim 1.290035846$$

Rounding to the nearest tenth gives us **1.3**.

Remarks: (1) We know that the sector is 1/12 of the circle because there are 360 degrees in a circle and 30/360 = 1/12.

(2) We can more formally find the area of the sector by using the following ratio:

	Sector	Circle
Angle	30	360
Area	x	48π

$$30/x = 360/48\pi$$
$$1440\pi = 360x$$
$$x = 1440\pi/360 = 4\pi$$

(3) If we were not asked to round to the nearest tenth, then we would grid in 1.29.

162

STRATEGY 28
COMPUTATION
OF SLOPES

Slope formulas are not given on the SAT. You should make sure that you know the following.

$$\text{Slope} = m = \frac{rise}{run} = \frac{y_2 - y_1}{x_2 - x_1}$$

Note: Lines with positive slope have graphs that go upwards from left to right. Lines with negative slope have graphs that go downwards from left to right. If the slope of a line is zero, it is horizontal. Vertical lines have **no** slope (this is different from zero slope).

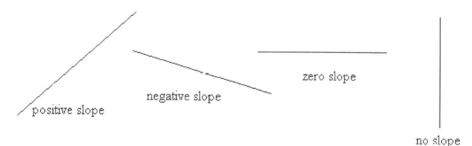

positive slope   negative slope   zero slope   no slope

You should also know the slope-intercept form of an equation of a line.

$$y = mx + b$$

m is the slope of the line and b is the y-coordinate of the y-intercept, ie. the point $(0, b)$ is on the line. Note that this point lies on the y-axis.

163

LEVEL 2: GEOMETRY

101. In an xy coordinate system, point B is located by beginning at A, moving 3 units up and then moving 2 units to the right. What is the slope of line AB ?

    (A) 0

    (B) $\dfrac{2}{3}$

    (C) 1

    (D) $\dfrac{3}{2}$

    (E) 2

* The slope of the line is m = rise/run = 3/2, choice (D).

LEVEL 3: GEOMETRY

102. If $y = 7x$ and the value of x is decreased by 3, then the value of y will be decreased by how much?

    (A) 1

    (B) 5

    (C) 7

    (D) 14

    (E) 21

* The slope of the line is 7 = 7/1. So, whenever x is increased by 1, y is increased by 7, or equivalently a decrease in x by 1 will decrease y by 7. So a decrease in x by 3 will decrease y by 7*3 = 21, choice (E).

An alternative method: Let's start by plugging in any value for x. Let's make x = 5. Then y = 7*5 = 35. Now let's decrease x by 3. So x is now 2. It then follows that y = 7*2 = 14. So y decreased by 35 − 14 = 21, choice (E).

LEVEL 4: GEOMETRY

103. Line k contains the point (2, 0) and has slope 3. Which of the following points is on line k ?

    (A) (0, 3)
    (B) (1, 3)
    (C) (2, 3)
    (D) (3, 3)
    (E) (4, 3)

The slope is 3 = 3/1. This means that an increase in x by 1 gives an increase in y by 3. So increasing x from 2 to 3 increases y from 0 to 3. Thus (3, 3) is on line k, choice (D).

* Remark: We can also say that an increase in y by 3 gives an increase in x by 1. It might make a bit more sense to use that in this problem since all answer choices have the same y coordinate. So in this case, increasing y from 0 to 3 increases x from 2 to 3.

For the advanced student: We can write an equation of the line in **point slope form**.

$$y - 0 = 3(x - 2)$$

We now distribute the right hand side to put the line into slope-intercept form.

$$y = 3x - 6$$

Now we can check if each point is on the line by substituting each point into the equation. For example, (2, 3) is not on the line because the equation 3 = 3*2 − 6 = 0 is false. On the other hand (3, 3) is on the line because 3 = 3*3 − 6 = 3 is true.

Point slope form: The point-slope form for an equation of a line is

$$y - y_0 = m(x - x_0)$$

where m is the slope of the line and (x_0, y_0) is a point on the line.

In the given problem m = 3, x_0 = 2 and y_0 = 0.

LEVEL 5: GEOMETRY

104. The slope of line segment AB is 5. If A has coordinates $(3, a)$ and B has coordinates $(7, b)$, what is the value of $b - a$?

(A) 20
(B) 10
(C) 5
(D) 0
(E) -5

* Geometric Solution: To get from 3 to 7 we travel right 4 units. So to get from a to b we must travel 4*5 = 20 units. So b − a = 20, choice (A).

Algebraic solution: Using the formula for slope we have

$$m = (b - a)/(7 - 3) = (b - a)/4.$$

Since we are given that m = 5, we have (b − a)/4 = 5/1. Cross multiplying gives us

$$b - a = 5*4 = 20.$$

Thus, the answer is choice (A).

LEVEL 5: GEOMETRY

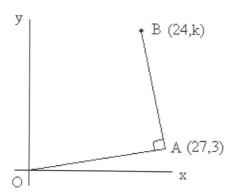

105. In the xy-plane above, $OA = AB$. What is the value of k ?

* To get from O to A we go up 3 units, right 27 units. So the slope of OA is 3/27 = 1/9. Since AB is **perpendicular** to OA, we have that the slope of AB is -9 = -9/1. Thus for every unit we move right along AB, we must move down 9 units. Equivalently, for every unit we move left along AB, we must move up 9 units. To get from 27 to 24 we must move left 3 units. Therefore we must move up 3*9 = 27 units. Since we're starting at 3, k = 3 + 27 = **30**.

Note: Parallel lines have the **same** slope. **Perpendicular lines** (lines which form right angles) have slopes that are **negative reciprocals** of each other. The reciprocal of 1/9 is 9/1 = 9 (and vice versa). The negative reciprocal of 1/9 is -9.

An algebraic solution using slopes: We can do all of this algebraically using the slope formula as follows.

The slope of OA is (3 − 0)/(27 − 0) = 3/27 = 1/9. So the slope of AB is -9 because OA and AB are perpendicular. We can also compute the slope of AB using the slope formula as follows.

$$m_{AB} = (k - 3)/(24 - 27) = (k - 3)/(-3)$$

Now set these equal to each other and solve for k (or guess and check).

$$(k - 3)/(-3) = -9$$
$$k - 3 = 27$$
$$k = \mathbf{30}$$

A solution using two applications of the Pythagorean Theorem: We form two right triangles and use the given points to write down three lengths as shown in the picture below.

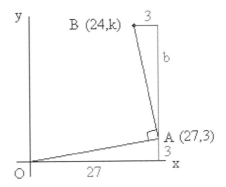

We can now find OA using the Pythagorean Theorem.

$$OA^2 = 27^2 + 3^2 = 738.$$

So OA = $\sqrt{738}$, and so AB = $\sqrt{738}$ also since OA = AB is given. Finally, we can use the Pythagorean Theorem one more time to find b.

$$3^2 + b^2 = AB^2$$
$$9 + b^2 = 738$$
$$b^2 = 729$$
$$b = 27$$

So k = 3 + 27 = **30**.

STRATEGY 29
TRIANGLES
INSIDE CIRCLES

*I*f a triangle (or triangles) is (are) inside a circle always check to see if any of the sides are radii of the circle. Remember that all radii of a circle have equal length.

LEVEL 2: GEOMETRY

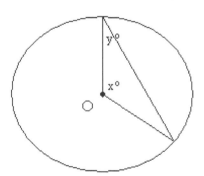

106. In the figure above, if $y = 32$ and O is the center of the circle, what is the value of x ?

* Note that the triangle is **isosceles**. In particular y is equal to the measure of the unlabeled angle. Therefore x = 180 − 32 − 32 = **116**.

Note: An **isosceles triangle** is a triangle with two congruent sides. In this case two of the sides are radii of the circle, and are thus congruent. Recall that the angles opposite these sides share the same relationship and therefore are also congruent.

LEVEL 5: GEOMETRY

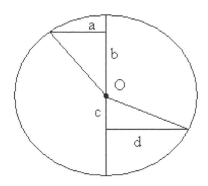

107. In the figure above, O is the center of the circle, the two triangles have legs of lengths a, b, c, and d, as shown, $a^2 + b^2 + c^2 + d^2 = 10$, and the area of the circle is $k\pi$. What is the value of k ?

* Notice that the hypotenuse of each triangle is a radius of the circle. By the Pythagorean Theorem, $a^2 + b^2 = r^2$ and $c^2 + d^2 = r^2$. So,

$$a^2 + b^2 + c^2 + d^2 = 2r^2$$

Since the left hand side of the above equation is also equal to 10, we have that $2r^2 = 10$, and therefore $r^2 = 5$.

Since the area of a circle is $A = \pi r^2$, we see that k = **5**.

STRATEGY 30
THE MEASURE OF AN EXTERIOR ANGLE OF A TRIANGLE

*T*he measure of an exterior angle of a triangle is the sum of the measures of the two opposite interior angles of the triangle.

LEVEL 2: GEOMETRY

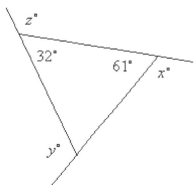

Note: Figure not drawn to scale.

108. In the figure above, what is the value of $x + y + z$?

Since there are 180 degrees in a triangle, it follows that the other interior angle is 180 − 32 − 61 = 87 degrees.

So we have

$$x = 87 + 32 = 119$$
$$y = 32 + 61 = 93$$
$$z = 87 + 61 = 148$$

So, x + y + z = 119 + 93 + 148 = **360**.

* **Quick trick:** A moment's thought will reveal that when we add x, y and z, we are adding each angle of the triangle twice. Since there are 180 degrees in a triangle, the answer is

2*180 = **360.**

So, the answer to this problem is independent of what any of the interior angles are actually equal to. In fact, none of those angles needed to be given at all.

If there were no angles given, you would have two options:

(1) Use the quick trick above.
(2) Choose **any** values for two of the angles, and proceed as in the simpler solution above.

LEVEL 5: GEOMETRY

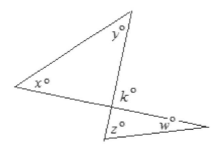

109. In the figure above, what is the average of x, y, z and w in terms of k ?

    (A) $\dfrac{k}{4}$

    (B) $\dfrac{k}{2}$

    (C) k

    (D) $2k$

    (E) $4k$

* k = x + y, and k = z + w. Thus x + y + z + w = 2k. The average of x, y, z and w is (x + y + z + w)/4 = 2k/4 = k/2, choice (B).

Remark: Note that the angle labeled k is an exterior angle of both triangles. We have used Strategy 30 twice here, once for each triangle.

STRATEGY 31
OPEN UP A CYLINDER TO GET A RECTANGLE

*W*hen we cut a cylinder down the height and open it up we get a rectangle. One side of the rectangle has the height of the cylinder as its length. The other side has the circumference of a base of the cylinder as its length.

LEVEL 5: GEOMETRY

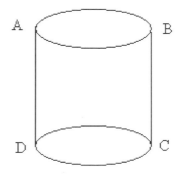

110. The figure shown above is a right circular cylinder. The circumference of each circular base is 18, the length of AD is 11, and AB and CD are diameters of each base respectively. If the cylinder is cut along AD, opened, and flattened, what is the length of AC to the nearest tenth?

* When we cut and unfold the cylinder as described we get the following rectangle.

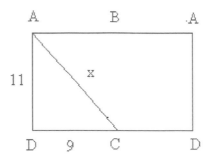

Notice that C is right in the middle of the rectangle. A common error would be to put C as one of the vertices. Note also that the length of the rectangle is 18 so that DC is 9. We can now use the Pythagorean Theorem to find AC.

$$x^2 = 9^2 + 11^2 = 81 + 121 = 202$$
$$x = \sqrt{202} \sim 14.2126704$$

Since the question asks for the answer to the nearest tenth, we grid in **14.2**.

Homework: Take a flat rectangular object such as a piece of paper or paper towel and put two sides together to form a cylinder. Open and close your cylinder and compare it to the two figures above until it is clear to you how the two figures relate to each other.

STRATEGY 32
TO MAKE SOMETHING LARGE MAKE SOMETHING ELSE SMALL (AND VICE VERSA)

LEVEL 2: NUMBER THEORY

111. A group of 182 parents is to be divided into committees with 3 or more parents on each committee. If each committee must have the same number of parents and every parent must be on a committee what is the maximum number of committees possible?

To get the maximum number of committees we will put as few parents as possible on each committee. Since there needs to be at least 3 parents on each committee, we will start by seeing if we can form committees of 3 parents.

$$182/3 \sim 60.67$$

We see that 182 is not divisible by 3, so we need to try a larger number of parents.

$$182/4 = 45.5$$
$$182/5 = 36.4$$
$$182/6 \sim 30.33$$
$$182/7 = 26$$

So 7 is the first positive integer greater than or equal to 3 that divides into 182 evenly. So the maximum number of committees possible is **26**.

* A quicker more advanced method: The **prime factorization** of 182 is

$$182 = 2*7*13$$

So the smallest number of parents we can put on each committee is 7 (we can't use 2 because there has to be at least 3 parents on a committee). Thus, the number of committees is 2*13 = **26**.

LEVEL 4: NUMBER THEORY

112. The sum of 12 positive even integers is 46. Some of these integers are equal to each other. What is the greatest possible value of one of these integers?

  (A) 26
  (B) 24
  (C) 22
  (D) 20
  (E) 18

* To make one of the integers as large as possible we will make the other eleven as small as possible. The smallest even positive integer is 2, so we make 11 of the integers 2. Thus the 12th integer is

$$46 - 11*2 = 46 - 22 = 24.$$

Thus the answer is choice (B).

Note: Since the word greatest appears and this is a Level 4 problem we can quasi-eliminate choices (A) and (E). So if we were to guess we would choose between (B), (C) and (D).

LEVEL 5: NUMBER THEORY

113. If $12 \leq x \leq 15$ and $8 \leq y \leq 11$, what is the greatest possible value of $\dfrac{3}{x-y}$?

* To make a fraction as large as possible, we make the denominator of the fraction as small as possible (while keeping it positive). So we want to make x − y as small as possible (but positive). To make x − y small, we make x as small as possible and y as large as possible. So we let x = 12 and y = 11. Then x − y = 12 − 11 = 1. Thus, 3/(x − y) = 3/1 = **3**.

A simpler but more tedious method: We compute 3/(x − y) when x and y are equal to each of the extreme values in the given ranges. The extreme values for x are 12 and 15. The extreme values for y are 8 and 11.

x	y	x − y	3/(x − y)
12	8	4	3/4 = .75
12	11	1	3/1 = 3
15	8	7	3/7 ~.42857
15	11	4	3/4 = .75

Notice that we tried all four possibilities using the extreme values for x and y. The last column shows that the greatest possible value of 3/(x − y) is **3**.

BONUS STRATEGIES
XIGGI'S FORMULA

The following simple formula can be used to find an average speed when two individual speeds for the same distance are known.

$$\text{Average Speed} = \frac{2(\text{Speed 1})(\text{Speed 2})}{\text{Speed 1} + \text{Speed 2}}$$

*Xiggi's formula is more widely known as the Harmonic Mean formula.

LEVEL 5: NUMBER THEORY

114. Sara ran a race of 800 meters in two laps of equal distance. Her average speeds for the first and second laps were 8 meters per second and 5 meters per second, respectively. What was her average speed for the entire race, in meters per second?

* We apply Xiggi's formula:

Average Speed = 2(8)(5)/(8 + 5) = 80/13 ~ 6.153846154. So grid in **6.15**.

An algebraic solution (in case you forget Xiggi's formula): We use the simple formula distance = rate * time. Let's put the given information into the following chart.

	Distance	Rate	Time
home to work	400	8	400/8 = 50
work to home	400	5	400/5 = 80
total	800		130

Note that we computed the times by using the formula in the form

time = distance/rate.

Finally, we use the formula in the form

rate = distance/time = 800/130 ~ 6.153846154.

So we grid in **6.15**.

Exercise for the advanced student: Use the formula d = rt to derive Xiggi's formula.

For a less straightforward application of Xiggi's formula see problem 43.

GENERALIZED PYTHAGOREAN THEOREM

The length of the long diagonal of a rectangular solid can be found by using the Generalized Pythagorean Theorem.

$$d^2 = a^2 + b^2 + c^2$$

where a, b and c are the length, width and height of the rectangular solid.

LEVEL 5: GEOMETRY

115. A cube with volume 64 cubic inches is inscribed in a sphere so that each vertex of the cube touches the sphere. What is the length of the radius, in inches, of the sphere?

180

The diameter of the sphere is the long diagonal of the cube.

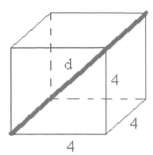

* In this problem, our rectangular solid is a cube. Thus a, b and c are all equal. Since the volume of the cube is 64, the length of a side of the cube is 4 (we get this by taking the cube root of 64). Thus, the diameter of the sphere is given by

$$d^2 = a^2 + b^2 + c^2 = 4^2 + 4^2 + 4^2 = 48 = 16*3.$$

So d = $4\sqrt{3}$, and the radius is r = d/2 = $2\sqrt{3}$.

Putting this in our calculator, we get r ~ 3.464101615 which we truncate (or round) to **3.46**.

Exercise for the advanced student: Draw a rectangular solid with sides of length a, b and c, and let the long diagonal have length d. Show geometrically that $d^2 = a^2 + b^2 + c^2$.

Hint: Apply the Pythagorean Theorem twice. The first time you will use two sides of the rectangular solid to get the length of the diagonal of the rectangle formed from those two sides. The second time you will use this diagonal together with the third side of the rectangular solid.

Congratulations! You are now much better prepared in SAT Math—and this preparation is going to show when you take your next practice tests and on the actual exam. You should be extremely proud of this accomplishment. You should feel much more confident walking into the exam.

Learning the strategies and doing the problems in this book will have boosted your SAT score and ultimately this means you will have a greater selection when choosing colleges.

Just by doing the problems in this book, understanding your errors, and redoing the problems you get wrong over and over until you can get them right on your own, you will be increasing your level of mathematical maturity, and increasing your SAT math score.

If you want to improve your score even more, you should reread the book focusing on the methods that you couldn't understand the first time around. Keep redoing those problems you can't quite get yourself until you can do them on your own. Once you can do the problems using the basic strategies presented here, try to solve them again using the more advanced methods presented. This will increase your mathematical maturity even further, and thus give an even greater improvement in your score.

After completing this book you should continue to do SAT Math problems for 10 to 20 minutes each day right up until the day of the SAT (but take off the day before the test). Try to stick mostly with problems created by the College Board and the author of this book. These will most closely reflect questions that will appear on the actual exam. Try to do problems that are at and slightly above your current ability level in each of the four major subject areas. Check www.theSATMathPrep.com frequently for free problems.

Try to complete at least four practice tests before taking the actual exam. For at least two of them you should take the whole test in one sitting (all Math, Critical Reading and Writing sections). Remember to follow the advice given in the introduction when preparing for the exam (Secret 3) and when actually taking the exam (Secret 4).

I really want to thank you for putting your trust in me. I realize how big a deal this is, and I want to assure you that you have made excellent use of your time by studying with this book. I wrote every sentence thinking how I can I increase your score with the minimum amount of effort. This book represents my ten plus years of experience as an SAT math tutor.

Nothing gives me greater pleasure then when I receive e-mails and phone calls from former students telling me how well they did on their SAT, or telling me that they made it into the college of their choice.

Writing this book has given me that same feeling of pleasure because I know that many more students are going to benefit from my experience even though I will never get to meet them all face to face.

Remember that you control your own destiny. Continue to work hard, and work smart. By using a little creativity you can usually accomplish any task you are given with a minimum amount of effort. Have confidence in yourself in everything you do and you will succeed. I wish you the best of luck on the SAT, on getting into your choice college, and in life.

Steve Warner, Ph.D.
steve@thesatmathprep.com

ACTIONS TO COMPLETE AFTER YOU HAVE READ THIS BOOK

1. Take another practice SAT

You should see a substantial improvement in your score.

2. Continue to practice SAT math problems for 10 to 20 minutes each day

Keep practicing problems of the appropriate levels until two days before the SAT. For additional practice use *320 SAT Math Problems arranged by Topic and Difficulty Level.*

3. Contact me for additional help

If you feel you need extra help that you cannot get from this book, please feel free to contact me at steve@thesatmathprep.com or post your question on my Facebook wall at www.facebook.com/thesatmathprep.

4. Critique this book

Leave a review on the site you purchased this book from; e.g. if you bought this book from Amazon, please give a genuine review of this book on the book's product page.

5. Visit my website www.thesatmathprep.com

You will find free content here that is periodically updated to help with your SAT math preparation

6. 'Like' my Facebook page

if you have not already done so. I would be very grateful!

About the Author

Steve Warner, a Staten Island (NY) native, earned his Ph.D. at Rutgers University in Pure Mathematics in May, 2001. While a graduate student, Dr. Warner won the TA Teaching Excellence Award.

After Rutgers, Dr. Warner joined the Penn State Mathematics Department as an Assistant Professor. In September, 2002, Dr. Warner returned to New York to accept an Assistant Professor position at Hofstra University. By September 2007, Dr. Warner had received tenure and was promoted to Associate Professor. He has taught undergraduate and graduate courses in Precalculus, Calculus, Linear Algebra, Differential Equations, Mathematical Logic, Set Theory and Abstract Algebra.

Over that time, Dr. Warner participated in a five year NSF grant, "The MSTP Project," to study and improve mathematics and science curriculum in poorly performing junior high schools. He also published several articles in scholarly journals, specifically on Mathematical Logic.

Dr. Warner has over 15 years of experience in general math tutoring and over 10 years of experience in SAT math tutoring. He has tutored students both individually and in group settings.

Currently Dr. Warner lives in Staten Island with his two cats, Achilles and Odin. Since the age of 4, Dr. Warner has enjoyed playing the piano—especially compositions of Chopin as well as writing his own music. He also maintains his physical fitness through weightlifting.

25380325R00101

Made in the USA
Lexington, KY
26 August 2013